ENGLISH AND ENGLISH LANGUAGE

Basic Skills

P. Wobu Buckroyd

Highly Experienced Senior Examiner

reac

BooksMu
Family his
Faxing**Ga**

Please
avoid
in pe

Bl
K
M
B
o
St
We
P

www.pearsonschoolsandfecolleges.co.uk

✓ Free online support
✓ Useful weblinks
✓ 24 hour online ordering

0845 630 33 33

Heinemann

Part of Pearson

Heinemann is an imprint of Pearson Education Limited, a company incorporated in England and Wales, having its registered office at Edinburgh Gate, Harlow, Essex, CM20 2JE. Registered company number: 872828

www.pearsonschoolsandfecolleges.co.uk

Heinemann is the registered trademark of Pearson Education Limited

Text © Pearson Education Limited 2010

First published 2010

14 13 12 11 10
10 9 8 7 6 5 4 3 2 1

British Library Cataloguing in Publication Data
A catalogue record for this book is available from the British Library on request.

ISBN 978 0 435151 30 0

Websites
The websites used in this book were correct and up-to-date at the time of publication. It is essential for tutors to preview each website before using it in class so as to ensure that the URL is still accurate, relevant and appropriate.

Edited by Jane Anson
Designed and produced by Kamae Design, Oxford
Cover design by Wooden Ark Studios, Leeds
Original illustrations © Pearson Education Limited 2010
Illustrated by Kamae Design and Rory Walker
Picture research by Virginia Stroud-Lewis
Cover photo © ImageSource
Printed and bound in Spain by Graficas Estella, S.L.

Acknowledgements
The author and publisher would like to thank the following individuals and organisations for permission to reproduce material in this book:

ppiv–v Getty Images News; pp2–3 Alamy/vario images GmbH & Co. KG/Bernhard Classen; p4 Courtesy of The Advertising Archives; p5 Getty Images/Tim Whitby; p7 Commercial Eye/Getty Images; p9 Corbis/PONGMANAT TASIRI/epa; p10 Getty Images; p14 Courtesy of The Advertising Archives; p17 Alex Segre/Alamy; p17 Alamy/marc macdonald; p20 BETWEEN THE EYES/THE KOBAL COLLECTION; p21 South West News Service; p22 Alamy/blickwinkel; p23 Alamy/blickwinkel; p25 Francis Wong Chee Yen. Shutterstock; p29 Alamy/Chris Wood; p31 Getty Images/Dave M. Benett; p31 Alamy/Roberto Soncin Gerometta; p33 Alamy/Roberto Soncin Gerometta; p35 Alamy/Bubbles Photolibrary; p36 News of the World; p40 Getty Images; p41 International Mammoth Committee; p43 Rex Features/Anne Katrin Purkiss; p45 Getty Images/Matt Cardy; p47 UNP/Rex Features; p50 Joe Gough. Shutterstock; p51 T.M.O.Buildings/Alamy; p53 South West News ServiceA; p55 Shutterstock/Ivonne Wierink; p56 Alamy/Manor Photography; p59 South West News Service; p63 Getty Images/Matthew Lewis; p64 Alamy/Picture Partners; p68 The Sun/News Group Newspapers/NI Syndication; p68 Manchester Evening News; p72 Photodisc. Photolink; p73 Londonstills.com/Alamy; p74 Londonstills.com/Alamy; p75 North Wind Picture Archives/Alamy; p76 Keith Martin; p77 Keith Martin; p82 Rex Features/Richard Young/; p83 Alamy/Ian Goodrick; p84 Alamy/Mode Images Limited; p86 South West News Service; p87 South West News Service; p88 South West News Service; p89 South West News Service; p93 Alamy/mediablitzimages (uk) Limited; p93 Alamy/Sally and Richard Greenhill; p95 Brendan Howard. Shutterstock; p97 Shutterstock/Bryan Busovicki; p99 Getty Images/Redferns/Andy Sheppard; p100 Janine Wiedel Photolibrary/Alamy; p105 Shutterstock/Monkey Business Images; p106 South West News Service; p110 Alamy/Richard G. Bingham II; p115 Alamy/National Trust Photolibrary/Jerry Harpur; p116 Getty Images/Thomas Niedermueller; p121 Alamy/Bubbles Photolibrary; p121 Alamy/Ace Stock Limited; p126 Getty Images/Clive Brunskill; p127 PA Photos/Neal Simpson/EMPICS Sport; p129 Alamy/Justin Kase zsixz; p129 Getty Images/Redferns/Dimitri Hakke; p132 Getty Images/Matt Cardy; p137 Rex Features/Hufton + Crow/View Pictures; p139 Getty Images/Photographer's Choice/Andrew Holt; p140 Alamy/Down Under Digital; p142 Sari Gustafsson/Lehtikuva/

Press Association Images; p145 Francis Specker/LANDOV/Press Association Images; p149 Getty Images/WireImage/Mark Allan/; p155 Getty Images/Taxi/Ken Lucas; p157 Alamy/Universal Images Group Limited; p159 Shutterstock/L T O'Reilly; p160 Shutterstock/2happy; p161 Shutterstock/2happy; p166 James Russell sport/Alamy; p167 Getty Images/Mark Dadswell.

'Thinning in the rain' by Carl Stroud, from the *Sun*, © 22 November 2009, used by permission of the *Sun* and NI Syndication. 'Boost your pecs appeal' by Peta Bee, from *The Times*, 8 December 2008, used by permission of *The Times* and NI Syndication. 'Seasonal savings' from *The Times*, © 8 December 2008, used by permission of *The Times* and NI Syndication. 'A jumbo feast to trumpet Elephant Day' from Reuters, used by permission of Reuters and PARS International. 'Blur go back to school' from the *Daily Star*, © 20 December 2008, used by permission of the *Daily Star* and Express Newspapers. BUPA advertisement used by kind permission of BUPA. 'Quacking gay love story' from the *Daily Express*, © 10 March 2009, used by permission of Express Newspapers. David Hayles, DVD review of 'Shifty' from *The Times Playlist*, © 22–28 August, 2009, used by permission of *The Times* and NI Syndication. 'Vegilante may nab allotment saboteur' by Allister Hagger, from the *Daily Express* website, © 2 September 2009, used by permission of Express Newspapers. 'Full stream ahead' by Chloe Lambert from *The Times*, © 19 March 2009, used by permission of *The Times* and NI Syndication. 'Dancing parrot mesmerises scientists' from the Orange website, May 2009, used by permission of Orange. 'Heaven on Earth' by Charlie Higson, from the *Daily Telegraph*, © 10 May 2009, used by permission of the *Daily Telegraph*. 'Mothers worth £33,000 a year' by Sarah O'Grady, from the *Daily Express*, © 16 March 2009, used by permission of Express Newspapers. 'Time to turn the cameras off Jade' by Carole Malone, from *News of the World*, 8 March 2009, used by permission of *News of the World* and NI Syndication. 'The 40,000 year old baby!' from the *Sun TV Magazine*, © 2–9 May, 2009, used by permission of the *Sun* and NI Syndication. 'Thanks, Carol' from the *Sun*, © 2 May 2009, used by permission of the *Sun* and NI Syndication. 'Nederlands Dans Theater 2' material from the Wales Millennium Theatre. Flyer © Wales Millennium Theatre, used by kind permission of the Wales Millennium Theatre. 'We've got it figured' from *News of the World*, © 28 December 2008, used by permission of *News of the World* and NI Syndication. 'Plod with the bod' by John Troup, from the *Sun*, © 6 December 2008, used by permission of the *Sun* and NI Syndication. 'The follies of Mad Jack' from the Orange website, used by permission of Orange. 'The definitive guide to the ugliest cars ever' from the Orange website, used by permission of Orange. 'It's a purr-fect crime' by Rod Chaytor, from the *Daily Mirror*, © 1 May 2009, used by permission of the *Daily Mirror* and Mirrorpix. 'Get me out of here' from *The People*, © 28 December 2008, used by permission of Mirrorpix. Benecol advertisement used by kind permission of McNeil Nutritionals Ltd – a Johnson & Johnson Company. 'You can sell this thing if it ain't got that bling' by Ben Ashford, from the *Sun*, © 22 November 2008, used by permission of the *Sun* and NI Syndication. Screech Owl Sanctuary leaflet, used by kind permission of the Screech Owl Sanctuary. 'Dinner tonight' by Lindsey Bareham, from *The Times*, © 8 December 2008, used by permission of *The Times* and NI Syndication. 'DLR to benefit from massive 2012 Games investment' from the *Metro*, 12 December 2008, used by permission of the *Metro* and Solo Syndication. Eden Project material, used by permission of THE EDEN PROJECT. 'Dinner tonight' by Lindsey Bareham, from *The Times*, © 16 December 2008, used by permission of *The Times* and NI Syndication. Material from the Events page of the St Albans Festival, used by permission of St Albans Council. 'Paul says fangs a lot' from the *Daily Express*, © 6 December 2008, used by permission of Express Newspapers. 'Your station at King's Cross' webpage, used by permission of FirstGroup plc. Headline: 'Phil the cracks! Players turning on Scolari' by Shaun Curtis and Paul Jiggins, from the *Sun*, used by permission of the *Sun* and NI Syndication. Headline: 'Bring back the beaver – he will save money and clean our rivers' by Valerie Elliot, from *The Times*, 8 March 2009, used by permission of *The Times* and NI Syndication. Headline: 'I canute believe It, my home is saved' by Aidan McGurran, from the *Daily Mirror* © 6 December 2008, used by permission of the *Daily Mirror* and Mirrorpix. Headline: 'Vince swims against the sea of sewage' by Kelvin Mackenzie, from the *Sun* 6 December 2008, used by permission of the *Sun* and NI Syndication. 'It's a plant officer' by John Coles, from the *Sun*, 6 December 2008, used by permission of the *Sun* and NI Syndication. 'Dopes' by Geoffrey Lakeman, from the *Daily Mirror* © 6 December 2008, used by permission of the *Daily Mirror* and Mirrorpix. 'Enjoy a great day out in Cornwall. Beautiful and inspiring places to visit in 2008' © Liz Luck/The National Trust, used by kind permission of The National Trust. 'Golf's cruellest game' from *Sky Sports Magazine*, used by permission of British Sky Broadcasting Group plc, Sky. 'We're worth every penny' by Jay Curson, from the *Guardian* 19 October 2002, used by permission of the *Guardian*. Copyright © Guardian News & Media Ltd 2002. 'How to …serve like Rafael Nadal' from *Sky Sports Magazine*, used by permission of British Sky Broadcasting Group plc.Sky. 'Birthday boy Bob keeps on building' by Miles Erwin, from the *Metro* © 7 September, used by permission of the *Metro* and Solo Syndication. 'Fun run conman' by Stephen White, from the *Daily Mirror* © 17 December 2008, used by permission of the *Daily Mirror* and Mirrorpix. '…and how did our 5ft 4in Tadpole become the best woman athlete in the world?' by Jenny Stocks, from the Daily Mail © 18 August 2009, used by permission of the *Daily Mail* and Solo Syndication. 'Explained Blu-ray' by Steve Davis, from *The Times* © 14–20 March 2009, used by permission of *The Times* and NI Syndication.

Every effort has been made to contact copyright holders of material reproduced in this book. Any ommissions will be rectified in subsequent printings if notice is given to the publishers.

Contents

How does this book work?

This book is designed to help students improve their basic skills in English and so raise their achievement in the AQA GCSE English and GCSE English Language exam (Unit 1).

The book breaks down the Assessment Objectives into their component parts. It then provides students with:

▶ guidance and teaching on the key skills that make the difference between grades G–C

▶ examples of students' work at grades G–C

▶ activities that allow students to reflect and improve on their learning

▶ the relevant mark-scheme descriptors together with guidance on what the examiners are looking for

▶ hints from an experienced Chief Examiner on how students can move up the grades.

The Student Book is accompanied by a Teacher Guide and an Active Teach CD-ROM, which together provide a wealth of print and digital teaching resources.

This book uses an approach based on many years of examining experience; it also draws on workshops, training sessions and revision courses with teachers and students.

Peter Buckroyd

How is the book structured?

The book is broken down into three sections:

▶ Reading ▶ Writing ▶ Exam practice.

The Reading and Writing sections are divided into chapters. These chapters relate either to complete Assessment Objectives, elements of Assessments Objectives or helpful deconstruction of the Assessment Objectives.

Each chapter is then broken down into manageable learning chunks (or notional lessons), each of which opens with its own learning objectives ('Your learning'). These introduce the skills, and then through stepped activities, modelling and examiner comments lead to a final task that allows students to tackle an exam-style question.

Regular Grade Studio activites help students understand what they need to do to improve their grades.

GradeStudio

Here are three student answers to the activity on pages 24–25. Read the answers together with the examiner comments, and then complete the final peer/self-assessment task.

G grade answer
Student A

Accurate information but not about either purpose or audience.

This web page is about parrots. It shows parrots dancing. The web page is directed at people who like reading about parrots.

A general point about audience but no supporting detail.

Examiner comment
This student makes one point about the audience but doesn't use any details to support the point. The first two sentences are just a waste of ink, because they don't answer the question! This answer is at the top of the G band.

D grade answer
Student B

Clear audience.

Point supported.

Two purposes.

This page is aimed at people who like reading about animals doing strange things. A parrot is dancing in the article and the picture. Its purpose is to entertain and amuse the readers because it's an unusual and funny story.

Supported in very general terms rather than with specific detail.

Examiner comment
There is one clear audience here and two purposes, but the supporting detail is mixed: the audience is clearly supported but the points about purpose need more precise detail. This is in the D band.

C grade answer
Student C

Purpose – to inform. Supported.

The purpose is to inform about some research done on parrots dancing; the scientist, Dr Patel, is quoted. It is also intended to amuse people who like funny stories. It is funny to find parrots dancing and the story was published in the 'quirky' category – meaning a strange and funny story. It may appeal to people who like to spend a lot of time on the internet, because it is from a website. It might also appeal to animal lovers because it is about a parrot.

Audience.

Supported.

More support for the same point.

Audience.

Audience.

Supported.

Examiner comment
This is a full and detailed answer, with each point supported by a detail from the text. It makes several points about purpose and several about audience, and therefore is right at the top of the C band.

Purpose and audience
To move up the grades, you need to make sure that everything you write is focused directly and clearly on the task. The more different points you can make, the better. Each point you make should be supported by a detail in the text.

Student A makes three points but only one of them is relevant to the task.

Student B's answer is better because it makes more than one relevant point and gives a little supporting detail.

Student C's answer is by far the best because it makes several clear points about both audience and purpose and then supports them.

Putting it into practice
Explain what you now know about:
- finding points to make about purpose
- finding points to make about audience
- answering the question
- finding precise support for the points you make
- what makes the difference between an G, D and C answer on purpose and audience.

In the future:
- practise finding purpose and audience with any text you come across
- you could practise with newspapers, magazines, pages from textbooks, letters and advertisements
- practise finding precise details to support the points you make
- for each type of text, give yourself about 10 minutes to practise this skill.

26   27

Most chapters conclude with the opportunity to read sample student answers and examiner comments on the final task in the chapter. These can be read by students before or after they grade themselves in the 'Peer/Self-assessment' activity.

Finally, each chapter concludes with an opportunity to reflect on what students have learnt and includes ideas for how they can practise those skills in the future.

At the end of the book there is a sample Foundation tier exam paper.

The AQA GCSE English and English Language specifications

This book is for students taking the AQA GCSE English and English Language Unit 1 exam. Although GCSE English and GCSE English Language are separate qualifications, the Unit 1 exam is common to both.

An overview of the specifications for both GCSE English and GCSE English Language can be found below and on the following pages.

GCSE English and GCSE English Language Unit 1

Here is an overview of the Unit 1 exam, which is common to both GCSE English and GCSE English Language. This book is designed to support this unit.

What is this unit worth?	40% of the total marks
How long is this exam?	2 hours
What is Section A of the exam?	Reading responses to non-fiction texts
What is Section A worth?	20% of the total marks
How long should you spend on Section A?	1 hour
What is Section B of the exam?	Two Writing responses
What is Section B worth?	20% of the total marks
How long should you spend on Section B?	1 hour

For full details, see the corresponding Heinemann Teacher Guide and AQA specifications.

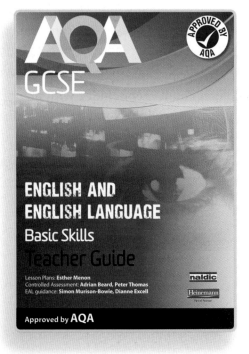

Unit 1: Resources from Heinemann

▶ Student Books – as well as this book, further grade-banded student books are available from Heinemann to support the teaching of Unit 1. We have developed the *Achieve an A** and *Achieve a C* student books so that you can pitch the learning at the appropriate level for your students.

▶ Teacher Guide – full colour lesson plans can be found in the corresponding Heinemann Teacher Guide, written by an experienced author and LA Adviser, Esther Menon. These lesson plans make use of and reference the BBC footage and other resources in the ActiveTeach CD-ROM as well as providing support for EAL students written by NALDIC (professional body of EAL teachers and advisors).

Each Teacher Guide is accompanied by a CD-ROM which contains the lesson plans as Word files, so they are fully customisable. If you have purchased both components these lesson plans can be uploaded into ActiveTeach.

> **Explains which assessment objectives are being covered.**

> **Advice from NALDIC on how to help EAL students access the content for each lesson.**

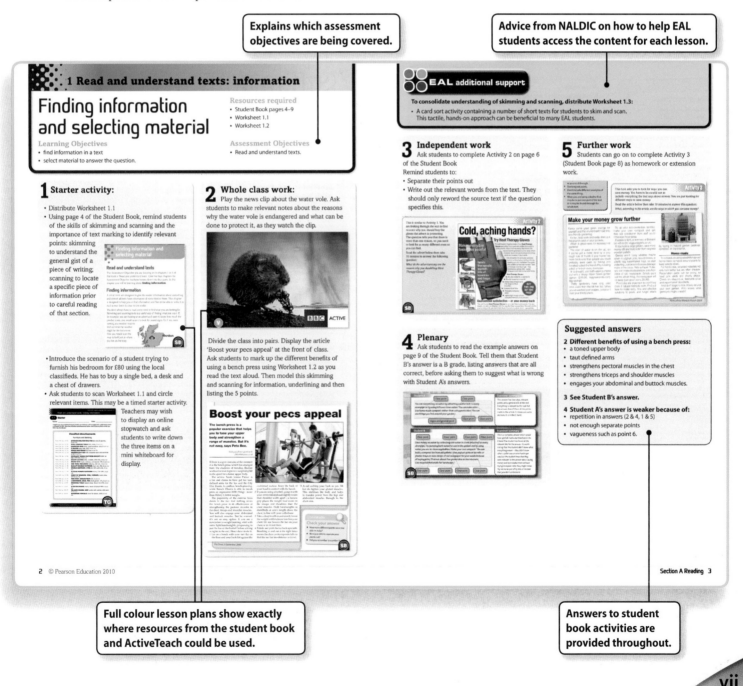

> **Full colour lesson plans show exactly where resources from the student book and ActiveTeach could be used.**

> **Answers to student book activities are provided throughout.**

► ActiveTeach CD-ROM – on-screen version of the Student Book together with BBC footage and other assets, including grade-improvement activities; additional video footage; worksheets and the full Teacher Guide. The resources and lesson plans are customisable and allow teachers to import their own resources.

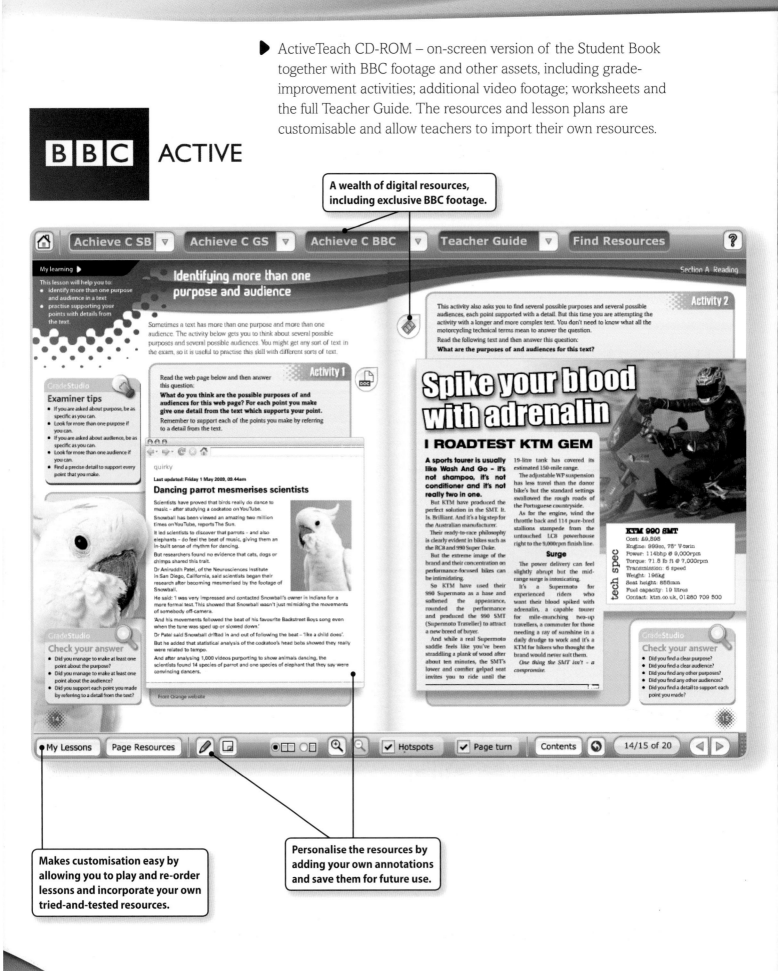

A wealth of digital resources, including exclusive BBC footage.

Makes customisation easy by allowing you to play and re-order lessons and incorporate your own tried-and-tested resources.

Personalise the resources by adding your own annotations and save them for future use.

GCSE English and GCSE English Language Unit 2

This is the Speaking and Listening Unit and is the same for GCSE English and GCSE English Language. It is worth 20% of the total marks and is Controlled Assessment. For full details, see the AQA specifications.

GCSE English and GCSE English Language Unit 3

There is commonality here between GCSE English and GCSE English Language, but for clarity they have been set out separately below. Unit 3 is Controlled Assessment and is worth 40% of the total marks.

GCSE English: Understanding and producing creative texts

This comprises:

- Understanding creative texts (literary reading) – worth 20% of the total marks.
- Producing creative texts (creative writing) – worth 20% of the total marks.

GCSE English Language: Understanding spoken and written texts and writing creatively

This comprises:

- Extended reading – worth 15% of the total marks.
- Creative writing – worth 15% of the total marks.
- Spoken Language Study – worth 10% of the total marks.

Controlled Assessment resources from Heinemann

This student book includes a section on the new Spoken Language Study. The Teacher Guides include comprehensive support for each of the three areas of Controlled Assessment. Written by experienced examiners and coursework moderators, each Controlled Assessment section includes:

- advice on the impact of the shift from coursework to Controlled Assessment

- specific guidance on all of the task types in the AQA Controlled Assessment Task Bank

- exemplar answers showing what kinds of responses you might expect to see

- suggestions for how you might approach, timetable and differentiate the Controlled Assessments.

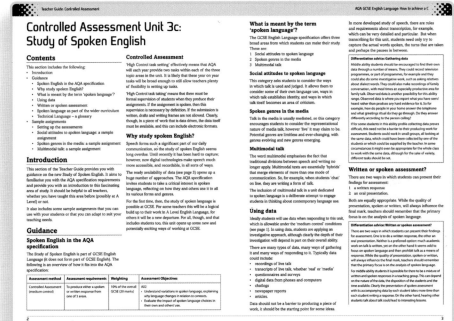

For full details, see the corresponding Heinemann Teacher Guide or AQA specifications.

This section of the book will help you to develop your Reading skills and get the best grade you can in your exam.

In this part of your course you will look at media and non-fiction texts. We all read media and non-fiction texts every day. This book will help you to understand, enjoy and analyse these texts.

The skills that you will work on in this book can be used with any texts that you read, in print or on screen. You don't just have to rely on English lessons to practise these skills.

This book focuses on the skills that you need to be successful in the exam. You will find a wide range of different texts and activities based around the kinds of questions that you might get in the exam. Practising these skills will help you to get the best grade you can.

Finding information

Skimming and scanning

Almost all texts have information of some kind in them. **Skimming** and **scanning** texts are useful ways of finding what you want.

If you were looking at an advert like the one here, what symbol would you scan it for to find the price of the product?

Activity 1

1 Skim the article opposite called 'Thinning in the Rain'. What is the article about?

2 Did you have to read the whole article to work this out? If not, which part of the text told you the answer?

Use these tips to help you.

- **Does the headline give you any clues?**

  The headline says George is losing his hair because of 'spins'.

- **What does the image tell you about what the article is about?**

  The photo shows George breakdancing.

- **Look for words that tell you what activity the article is about.**

  The word 'head-spins' appears several times.

Activity 2

1 Look again at the 'Thinning in the Rain' article below.

2 List **five** different things that the article tells you about George Sampson.
Number them 1 to 5. An example has been done for you.

1. *George Sampson is going bald because he spins on his head too much.*
2. _____
3. _____
4. _____
5. _____

Thinning In The Rain

EXCLUSIVE by CARL STROUD

'TALENT' STAR GEORGE LOSING HAIR IN SPINS

Britain's Got Talent winner George Sampson has had to ditch his trademark head-spinning dance move – as the friction is making him go bald.

The 15-year-old breakdancer has performed so many Singing In The Rain routines he has worn away a huge amount of hair.

Concerned mum Lesley has now warned him off the stunt.

She said: "I've told George not to do any more head-spins. He's losing his hair and if he doesn't stop now, it'll never grow back."

The star won £100,000 on the ITV1 show in May after honing his moves on the streets of Manchester.

George admitted: "I'm laying off the head-spins for the time being.

Crucial

"I've had to. I've been doing them for years. My hair's thinning on top and I don't want to lose it for good."

The young star's debut single 'Get Up On The Dance Floor' comes out on Monday – and he releases DVD *Access 2 All Areas* in the next month.

George said the single was "crucial" to what he does next. He added: "If it does well I'm going to make an album. If more people buy the DVD I'll focus on dancing again."

The *Sun* told in June how George suffers from rare spine problem Scheuermann's disease – even though he flips on to his back during his routine.

sun

c.stroud@the-sun.co.uk

Finding the right section

Re-cap

In the last lesson you learned how to skim and scan a text to find information. Sometimes the information you need is just in one part of a text. In these cases you have to find that section first.

Activity 1

1. Look at the article opposite called 'Boost your pecs appeal'.

2. First, scan the text to find the section that lists the advantages of using a bench press. If you are unsure which section is the right one, then you should read the whole text carefully to double-check.

3. Now that you have found that section, list the **five** different benefits of using a bench press. Remember to number your points!

1. _____

2. _____

3. _____

4. _____

5. _____

Don't worry if you don't know what all the words mean. The task is to find the relevant points, not to understand what everything means.

Boost your pecs appeal

THE TIMES

If there is a gym exercise of the moment it is the bench press, which has emerged from the shadows of trendier, flashier workout moves to prove a surprising hit in the quest for a toned upper body.

The actress Sarah Jessica Parker is a fan and claims to have got her taut, defined arms for the *Sex and the City* film thanks to endless bench-pressing, while Barack Obama is able to bench press an impressive 200lb (91kg) – more than Hillary Clinton weighs.

The popularity of the exercise boils down to the fact that nothing rivals the bench press in its effectiveness at strengthening the pectoral muscles in the chest, triceps and shoulder muscles.

You will also engage your abdominal and buttock muscles. But be warned: it's not an easy option. If you are a newcomer to weight training, start with some light handweights, progressing to just the bar of the barbell before adding weights to the end. Here's how to do it:

1 Lie on a bench with your feet flat on the floor and your back flat against the cushioned surface. Keep the back of your head in contact with the bench.

2 If you are using a barbell, grasp it with your arms extended and slightly wider than shoulder width apart – a narrow grip places the weight load more on the triceps and shoulders than the chest muscles. Hold handweights or dumbbells at arm's length above the chest, in line with your collarbone.

3 Take a deep breath in and slowly lower the weight until it almost touches your chest. Do not bounce the bar on your chest or let it rest there.

4 Exhale and push the bar back upwards. Breathing in and out at the right times means the chest cavity expands fully so that the bar has less distance to travel.

5 Avoid arching your back as you lift but do tighten your gluteal muscles. This stabilises the body and helps to transfer power from the legs and abdominal muscles through to the chest area.

Send your fitness questions to fitness@thetimes.co.uk

Check your answer

GradeStudio

In your answer to Activity I:
- Did you scan the text to find the right section?
- Did you list the five benefits of using the bench press?
- Were all your points different?
- Did you number your points I to 5?

Your learning

This lesson will help you to:

- find information in a text
- select material to answer a question.

Re-cap

In the last lesson, you found information from a longer text. You did this by scanning the text first to find the right section.

Sometimes, though, you have to read the whole text in order to find the information you need.

Activity 1

1 Read this article about seasonal savings.

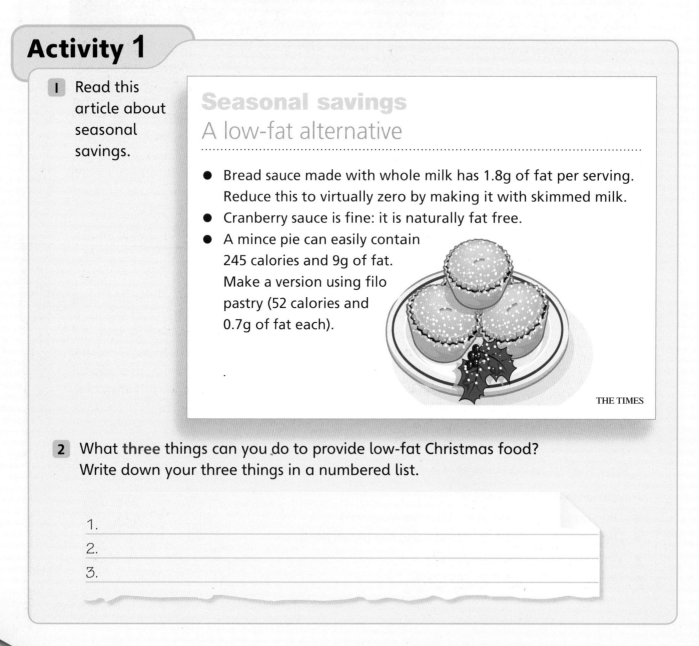

Seasonal savings
A low-fat alternative

- Bread sauce made with whole milk has 1.8g of fat per serving. Reduce this to virtually zero by making it with skimmed milk.
- Cranberry sauce is fine: it is naturally fat free.
- A mince pie can easily contain 245 calories and 9g of fat. Make a version using filo pastry (52 calories and 0.7g of fat each).

THE TIMES

2 What **three** things can you do to provide low-fat Christmas food? Write down your three things in a numbered list.

1. _____
2. _____
3. _____

Activity 2

1 Read the article about National Elephant Day.

2 List **five** things that elephants did on National Elephant Day.

3 Remember to number your list I to 5.

THE TIMES

A jumbo feast to trumpet Elephant Day

Chiang Mai Elephants tuck in to a variety of fruit, left at a buffet laid out for them on National Elephant Day in Thailand yesterday.

Huge bunches of bananas and tonnes of sugar cane were on the menu for the all-you-can-eat treat at the Maesa Elephant Camp sanctuary in the northern province of Chiang Mai.

More than 70 elephants took part in the festivities, which have been held since 1998, when the Government declared March 13 National Thai Elephant Day.

Hundreds of tourists watched the animals as they paraded around the camp, played sports matches and even painted pictures.

Elephants at the sanctuary are taught to play sports such as football, bowls, baseball and basketball.

One elephant used its trunk to blow darts to burst balloons.

The elephant is Thailand's national animal and government officials hope that events such as National Elephant Day will make people revere them as it tries to conserve its elephant population, now around 4,500.

'The Government declared March 13 to be National Elephant Day. We hold the ceremony to let people know how important Thai elephants are,' Chuchart Kallamapichit, the owner of the Maesa Elephant Camp, said. (*Reuters*)

Check your answer

GradeStudio

In your answer to Activity 2:
- Did you find five things?
- Were all your points different?
- Did you number your points I to 5?

Your learning

This lesson will help you to:

- practise an exam-style question
- compare your own answer with other students' answers.

Activity 1

This activity asks you to look for information about the band Blur.

- To get top marks, you need to find all the points and make them clearly.
- Always underline the points in pencil as you are reading the text.
- Make sure you don't repeat the same points.
- Remember that the information you are being asked to find might be in one part of the text or throughout the whole text.

1 Read the article about the band Blur.

2 Answer the question below in 10 minutes.

What information is given in the article about Blur and its members?

Blur go back to school...

EXCLUSIVE

RE-FORMED Britpop heroes Blur will go back to college to play their first gig since becoming best buddies again.

I can reveal the guys will road-test their live show at Goldsmiths College, the London art school where they formed in 1989, ahead of their huge Hyde Park dates.

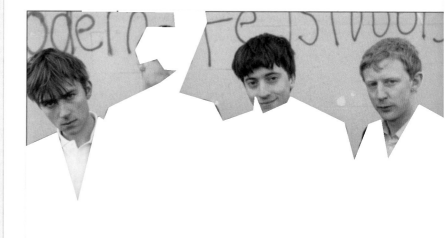

BACK TO THE FUTURE: The boys from Blur are all pals again

Frontman **Damon Albarn**, 40, bassist **Alex James**, 41, guitarist **Graham Coxon**, 39, and drummer **Dave Rowntree**, 40, pictured here in their heyday, haven't played together since 2000.

Strained relations between Damon and Graham caused the band to split but earlier this month they announced gigs for July 2009 in the London park.

A source said: 'Blur did a secret gig at Goldsmith's before their greatest hits tour back in the day, so it seemed like the ideal place to iron out any creases in the set before they hit Hyde Park. They are looking at slotting something in around June back at their old art stomping ground.

'But they're also talking about some other warm-ups around the UK.' Damon has mentioned playing in his home town of Colchester as well as Wolverhampton.

Memories

The Country House lads will also take Glastonbury back to its traditional rock 'n' roll roots with a headline performance at Worthy Farm.

My source continued: 'A lot of bands have got back together for the money – but with Blur it really is all about breathing new life into the old songs that hold massive memories for a generation.

'They want to give something back to the people who supported them. Goldsmiths will be one of the moments of the year for indie fans who manage to get a ticket.'

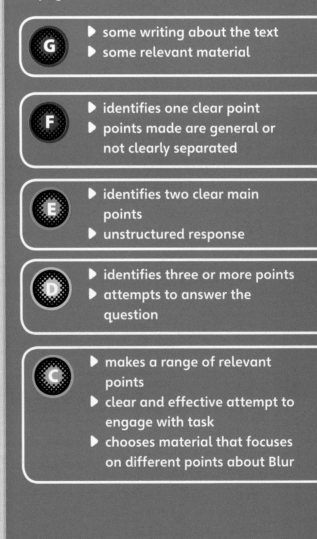

Peer/Self-assessment activity

1 Check your answer to the assessment activity. Did you:
 • include all the different points you could find
 • avoid repetition and examples of the same thing
 • make your answer clear and detailed?
2 Now grade your answer using the mark scheme below. First, read the sample answers to this task on pages 12–13.

G
 ▶ some writing about the text
 ▶ some relevant material

F
 ▶ identifies one clear point
 ▶ points made are general or not clearly separated

E
 ▶ identifies two clear main points
 ▶ unstructured response

D
 ▶ identifies three or more points
 ▶ attempts to answer the question

C
 ▶ makes a range of relevant points
 ▶ clear and effective attempt to engage with task
 ▶ chooses material that focuses on different points about Blur

Here are three student answers to the activity on pages 10–11.
Read the answers together with the examiner comments and then complete the final peer/self-assessment task.

Student A

Not relevant to the task.

Another general point.

Blur is a pop group that was famous in the 1990s after they had got together in 1989. The members of the group have got back together again and are going to perform in Hyde Park.

General point about the group.

Examiner comment

This answer begins with a point not in the article. Two general points are made but they are not the specific points made in the article. This is in the G band.

Student B

Two points made.

Blur is a pop group which was formed in 1989 and have got back together again. The members of the group are Damon Alborn, Alex James, Graham Coxon and Dave Roundtree. They are going to perform in Hyde Park.

Another point.

Four members of group mentioned but two names miscopied and so not accurate.

Examiner comment

This answer has several main points. Everything is relevant to the task, but the answer doesn't have all the points made in the article; it misses out some sections. The misspelling of the names means that it is not entirely accurate. It attempts the task but doesn't do it clearly and accurately. It is in the E band.

Student C

Relevant information.

Detailed information.

Detailed information.

> The pop group Blur, formed in 1989, consists of frontman Damon Albarn (40), bassist Alex James (41), guitarist Graham Coxon (39) and drummer Dave Rowntree (40). Having got back together, they will play at Goldsmiths College where they formed, before playing in Hyde Park in 2009. They might play at other places like Colchester, Wolverhampton and Glastonbury.

Examiner comment

This is a full answer which would have got full marks. The student has found all the relevant bits for the answer and put them together without wasting words. It gets full marks and is well into the C band.

Finding information

To move up the grades, you need to make a wider range of points and to be more exact and specific in the points you make. This is clearly shown in the difference between the answers from Student A and Student C.

For a C grade, you need to find all the sections of the text that give you information. Then you need to write your points clearly, making sure that each is relevant for the answer.

Putting it into practice

Explain what you now know about:
- finding information in texts
- separating the points
- answering the question
- what makes the difference between grade G, E and C answers on these types of questions.

In the future:

- practise this exercise with any information text you come across
- you could practise with newspapers, magazines, pages from textbooks, letters and advertisements
- for each type of text, give yourself about 10 minutes to practise this skill.

Identifying purpose and audience

Your learning

This lesson will help you to:

- identify the purpose of a text
- identify the audience of a text
- comment on purpose and audience.

What is purpose?

The **purpose** is the main reason for the text – what it is for. For example, the purpose of an advert is to **persuade** people to buy something.

What is audience?

The **audience** is who the text is aimed at – who it is for. For example, an advert for trainers that includes a photo of young people tells us that the trainers are for young people. You can pick up clues about who the audience is by looking at the pictures and the language.

Look at the advert below. Who do you think it is aimed at?

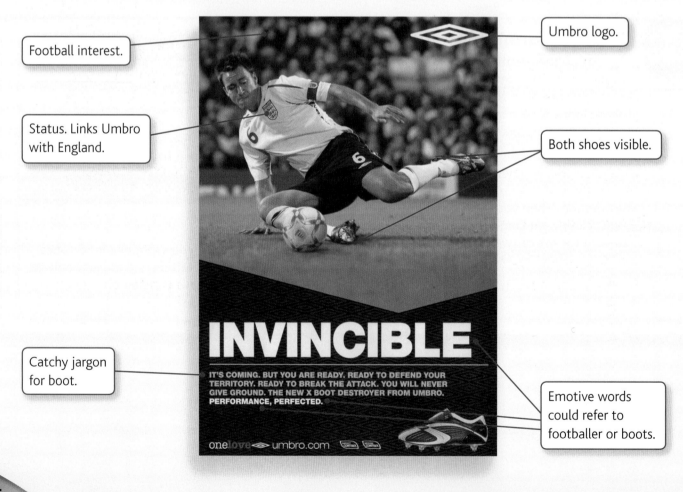

Football interest.

Umbro logo.

Status. Links Umbro with England.

Both shoes visible.

Catchy jargon for boot.

Emotive words could refer to footballer or boots.

INVINCIBLE

IT'S COMING. BUT YOU ARE READY. READY TO DEFEND YOUR TERRITORY. READY TO BREAK THE ATTACK. YOU WILL NEVER GIVE GROUND. THE NEW X BOOT DESTROYER FROM UMBRO. PERFORMANCE, PERFECTED.

onelove umbro.com

Activity 1

1. Read texts A–E on pages 16 and 17.
2. For each text, choose what kind of text it is from the box on the right.

Text type
- letter of complaint
- advertisement
- informal text
- brief article
- informative text

3. Now match each text to the correct purpose from the box on the right.

Purpose of the text
- to persuade
- to inform
- to communicate
- to complain
- to entertain

4. Now choose the correct audience for each text from the box on the right.

Audience for the text
- UK residents
- a friend
- a manufacturer
- nurses
- readers of a tabloid newspaper

5. Write you answer in a table like this.

Text	Text type	Purpose	Audience
A	Letter of complaint	To complain	A manufacturer
B			
C			
D			
E			

6 Culvert Avenue
Sumtown
Derbs AZ3 9QR

4 May 2009

The Mail Order Department
Dudgifts
4 High Street
Gormansville G14 8BV

Dear Sirs,

I ordered two plates from you for my wife's birthday (Ref. X32 409) but when they arrived they were smashed. There was no fragile notice on the package and the packaging itself was very flimsy. This is disgraceful.

Broken plates are no use either to me or to my wife.

Please either send me two more of what I ordered, properly packaged this time, or refund my money.

I look forward to a prompt reply.

Yours faithfully,

D. Gruntled

Text B

We've been operating longer than the NHS and have 450 established care homes globally

Many of our nurses progress to junior or senior sister roles & management roles

We re-invested over £46m back into the business in 2008

Bupa is recognised to have an industry high of top performing care homes.

Change the way you think about our care homes

Job satisfaction is at a record 85.1% high

We have opportunities to work in the UK, Spain, Australia & New Zealand

Last year we invested £4m in 22,000 training opportunities

Nurses

Job Opportunities Nationwide

Being a Nurse at Bupa is both professionally and personally rewarding. Bupa continues to invest in the refurbishment of homes and building of new homes and we are continuing to invest in training for our valued care home staff.

We invested £4 million in training in 2008 and we are on track to invest more in 2009. This investment ensures that our residents receive high, consistent levels of quality care they deserve in a Bupa home.

With 87% of Bupa homes rated good or excellent by the Care Quality Commission, we are proud of our teams and recognise the value each one of our employees makes to the welfare of the residents, with 85.1% of staff being satisfied with us as an employer.

Our Nurses receive the best training and development opportunities to help them move on in their careers, as well as recognition for doing what they do best, caring.

So, change the way you think about the future and contact Sarah Cashman on 0113 381 6131, email cashmans@bupa.com

Bupa Care Homes
Everyday Heroes
www.bupacarehomes.co.uk

Bupa

Text C

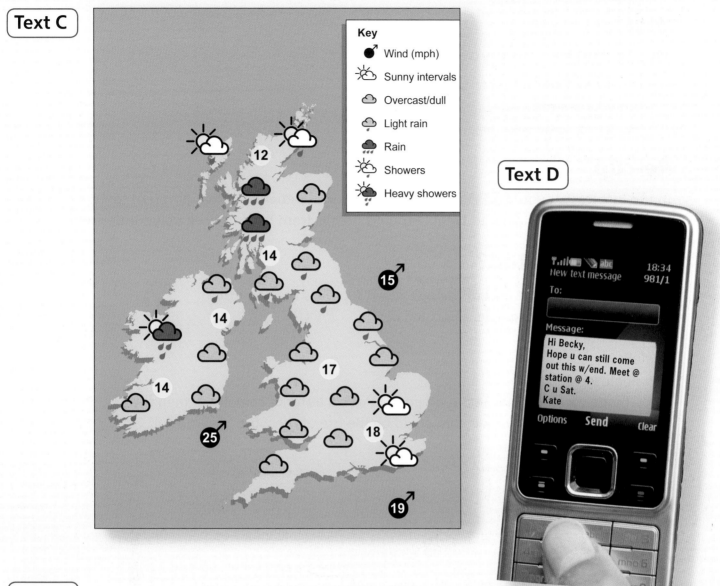

Key

- 🜚 Wind (mph)
- ⛅ Sunny intervals
- ☁ Overcast/dull
- 🌦 Light rain
- 🌧 Rain
- 🌦 Showers
- 🌧 Heavy showers

12

14

14

15

14

14

17

25

18

19

Text D

📶 🔋 abc   18:34
New text message   981/1
To:

Message:
Hi Becky,
Hope u can still come
out this w/end. Meet @
station @ 4.
C u Sat.
Kate

Options   **Send**   Clear

Text E

Quacking gay love story

It was hoped that feathers would fly when two rare male blue ducks were introduced to the only female of their species in Britain.

Ben and Jerry were meant to fall for Cherry and help produce some much-needed ducklings.

Instead, the two drakes only had eyes for each other – and have been inseparable ever since.

Daily Express

Paul Stevens, warden of Arundel Wetland Centre in West Sussex, said: 'To our surprise the two males really took to each other. It would have been nice to get a last clutch of eggs from Cherry, but Ben and Jerry do make a lovely couple.'

TV wildlife expert Chris Packham said: 'Ducks are one of the few species that show homosexual behaviour regularly.'

But the gay love story does nothing to help the endangered blue duck, with just 2,500 now left in their native New Zealand.

The gay blue ducks Ben and Jerry yesterday

Your learning

This lesson will help you to:

- find details from a text to support the point you are making.

Re-cap

In the last lesson, you worked out the purpose and audience of five different texts.
In the exam, you will need to be able to find details from texts to back up your decisions.

What is a detail?

A **detail** means a short part of the text which supports the point that
you are making. For example, this could be:

- a sentence
- a phrase
- a single word.

If you made the point that Text A on page 16 was a letter of complaint, then the
detail from the text to support this would be the use of the word 'disgraceful'.

> 6 Culvert Avenue
> Sumtown
> Derbs AZ3 9QR
>
> 4 May 2009
>
> The Mail Order Department
> Dudgifts
> 4 High Street
> Gormansville G14 8BV
>
> Dear Sirs,
>
> I ordered two plates from you for my wife's birthday (Ref. X32 409) but
> when they arrived they were smashed. There was no fragile notice on the
> package and the packaging itself was very flimsy. This is disgraceful.

The examiner wants to know what bits of text you are looking at when you make a
point, so you should always include one detail from the text to support the point that
you are making.

Activity 1

1 Read Texts A–E on pages 16 and 17 again.

2 For each text, give a reason why you matched it to the purpose that you did. An example has been done for you, based on Text A.

> **Text A**
>
> This is *a complaint because it uses the word 'disgraceful'*.

Each time you make a point you should give a detail to support the statement. 'Because' is a very useful word to use to do this.

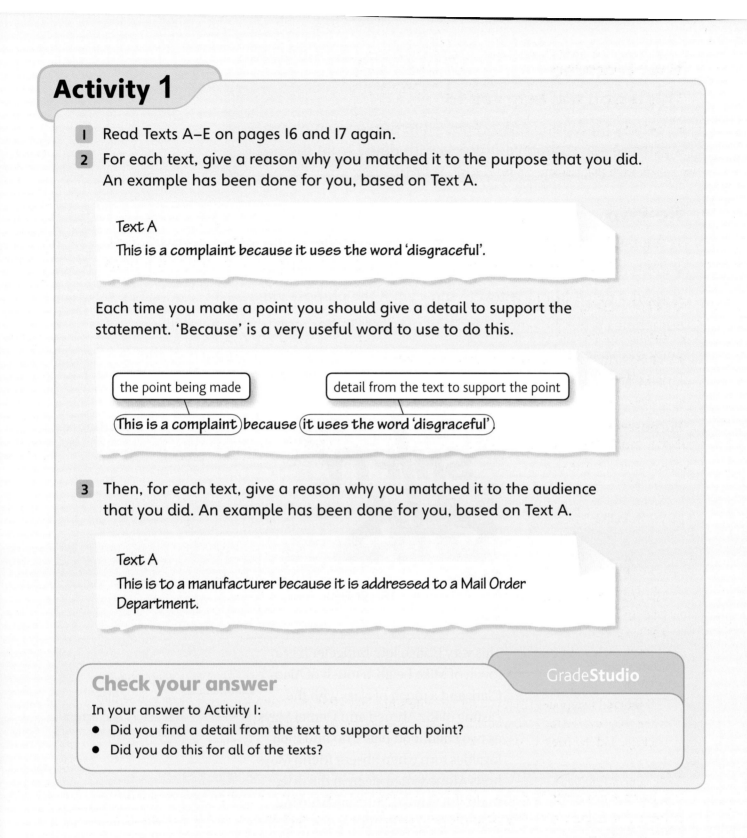

the point being made		detail from the text to support the point

This is a complaint because it uses the word 'disgraceful'.

3 Then, for each text, give a reason why you matched it to the audience that you did. An example has been done for you, based on Text A.

> **Text A**
>
> This is *to a manufacturer because it is addressed to a Mail Order Department*.

Check your answer

GradeStudio

In your answer to Activity 1:
- Did you find a detail from the text to support each point?
- Did you do this for all of the texts?

Your learning

This lesson will help you to:

- identify more than one purpose and audience in a text
- practise supporting your points with detail from the text.

Re-cap

In the last lesson, you looked at different texts and:

- used a detail from the text to show who the audience was
- used a detail from the text to show what the purpose was.

Sometimes a text has more than one purpose and/or more than one audience.

Look at this text about a recent DVD. The labels show you which parts of the text you could use to make a comment about purposes and audiences.

Purposes

Audiences

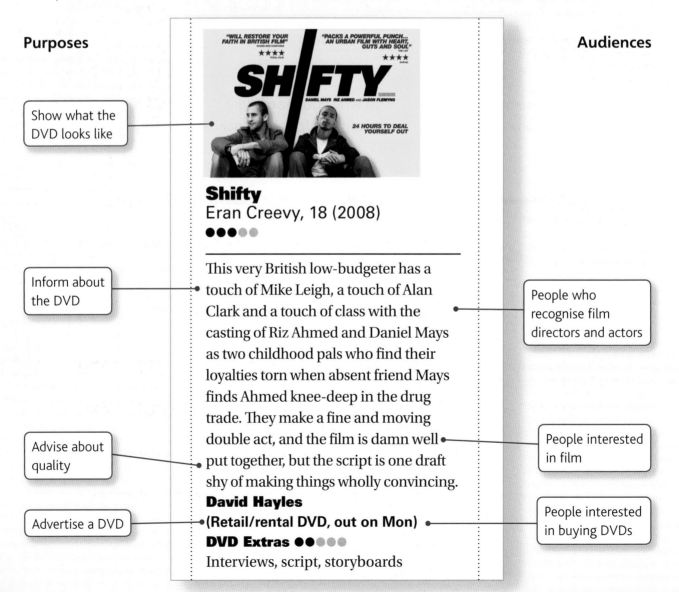

Show what the DVD looks like

Inform about the DVD

Advise about quality

Advertise a DVD

Shifty
Eran Creevy, 18 (2008)
●●●●○○

This very British low-budgeter has a touch of Mike Leigh, a touch of Alan Clark and a touch of class with the casting of Riz Ahmed and Daniel Mays as two childhood pals who find their loyalties torn when absent friend Mays finds Ahmed knee-deep in the drug trade. They make a fine and moving double act, and the film is damn well put together, but the script is one draft shy of making things wholly convincing.
David Hayles
(Retail/rental DVD, out on Mon)
DVD Extras ●●○○○
Interviews, script, storyboards

People who recognise film directors and actors

People interested in film

People interested in buying DVDs

Activity 1

Read the text below. What is the purpose of this text? Try to think of more than one. Who is the audience?

---

http://www.express.co.uk/posts/view/124388/Vegilante-may-nab-allotment-saboteur

HOME > NEWS / SHOWBIZ > UK NEWS

UK NEWS

VEGILANTE MAY NAB ALLOTMENT SABOTEUR

POLICE are hunting a jealous serial saboteur after attacks on prize crops at two allotments tended by 70 growers.

The vandal uses a metal spike and weed killer to attack flowers and vegetables, including pumpkins and cabbages.

Officers have been called to the allotments three times this year.

Now growers are considering using 'vegilantes' to patrol their plots.

The latest victim is Tony Mason, 67.

The award-winner spent months tending his carrots, cabbages and pumpkins ahead of the Torquay Allotment Association Show.

But the day before the event on Saturday he found his prized pumpkins had been punctured and his cabbages impaled by a spike.

However, the judges took pity on him and awarded him two first prizes despite the damage.

He said: 'I don't know what's up with these sick people. I can't believe they would do this to me.'

Activity 2

1 Read the article 'Full stream ahead!' What is the purpose of the article?
Choose from the list below. You can choose more than one purpose.

- inform
- explain
- complain
- advise
- persuade
- advertise
- describe

2 For each word you chose, write a sentence giving a detail from the text to
support your point. You could use the following sentence structure:

> *One of the purposes of this text is to* _____
> *because* _____ .

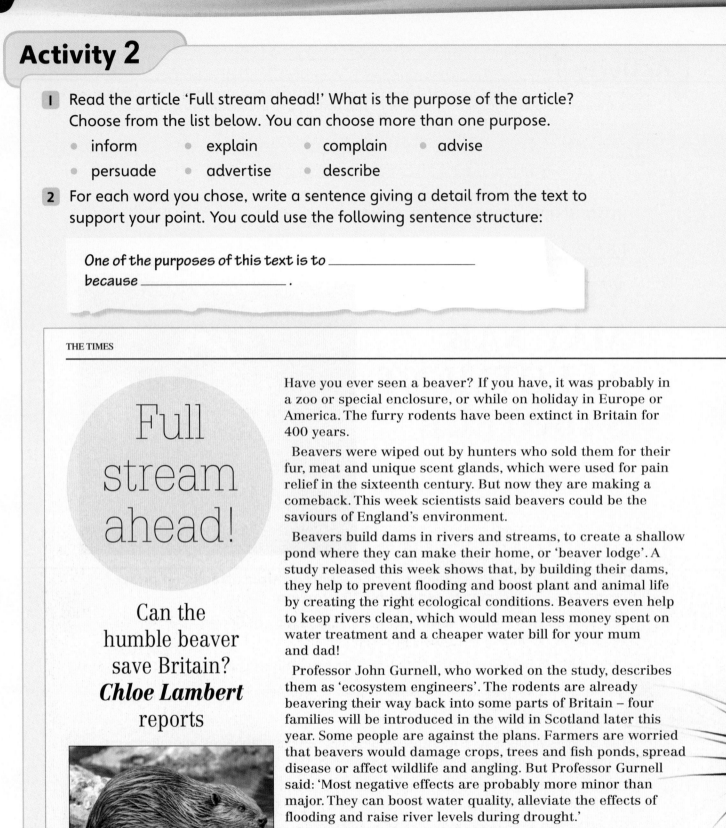

THE TIMES

Full stream ahead!

Can the humble beaver save Britain?
Chloe Lambert reports

Have you ever seen a beaver? If you have, it was probably in a zoo or special enclosure, or while on holiday in Europe or America. The furry rodents have been extinct in Britain for 400 years.

Beavers were wiped out by hunters who sold them for their fur, meat and unique scent glands, which were used for pain relief in the sixteenth century. But now they are making a comeback. This week scientists said beavers could be the saviours of England's environment.

Beavers build dams in rivers and streams, to create a shallow pond where they can make their home, or 'beaver lodge'. A study released this week shows that, by building their dams, they help to prevent flooding and boost plant and animal life by creating the right ecological conditions. Beavers even help to keep rivers clean, which would mean less money spent on water treatment and a cheaper water bill for your mum and dad!

Professor John Gurnell, who worked on the study, describes them as 'ecosystem engineers'. The rodents are already beavering their way back into some parts of Britain – four families will be introduced in the wild in Scotland later this year. Some people are against the plans. Farmers are worried that beavers would damage crops, trees and fish ponds, spread disease or affect wildlife and angling. But Professor Gurnell said: 'Most negative effects are probably more minor than major. They can boost water quality, alleviate the effects of flooding and raise river levels during drought.'

Should beavers return to England, the riverbanks in the Weald of Kent, the New Forest, Bodmin Moor, the Lake District and the Forest of Bowland have all been chosen as potential new homes.

Activity 3

Now you need to think about the different possible audiences that a text might have. Remember, the audience is who the text is aimed at.

1 Look again at the article 'Full stream ahead!'

2 Now decide which of the possible audiences in the list below applies to the article.

- old people
- people interested in animals
- pet lovers
- young readers
- journalists

3 For each possible audience you choose, write a sentence giving a detail from the text to support your point.

Check your answer

In your answers to Activities 2 and 3:
- Did you find more than one audience and purpose in the text?
- For each audience, did you write a sentence including a detail from the text?

Beavers have a danger signal that they use when they are startled while swimming. The beaver quickly dives under the surface while slapping the water with its broad tail. The sound can be heard above and below the water. It alerts other beavers, which dive and may not emerge for some time. They can stay under water for as long as 15 minutes.

Beavers are nocturnal. They build their dams during the night, using their powerful front teeth and front paws to carry mud, stones and wood. The biggest beaver dam recorded was 850m long, in Canada.

More than 13,000 years ago, the giant beaver stalked North America. The size of a black bear, it was one of our largest rodents but has long been extinct.

There are two species of beaver: the European and the North American. The European is up to 1m long and weighs about 20kg.

Your learning

This lesson will help you to:

- practise an exam-style question
- assess your own answer by comparing it with what other students have written.

Activity 1

1. Read this web page about a dancing parrot.

2. What do you think are the possible purposes and audiences for the web page?

3. For each point you make, give one detail from the text to support your point. Spend 10 minutes answering this question.

---

http://www.orange.co.uk/news/quirkies/default.htm?om=storyitem/storyId=3303380

Last updated: Friday 1 May 2009, 09.44am

Dancing parrot mesmerises scientists

Scientists have proved that birds really do dance to music – after studying a cockatoo on YouTube.

Snowball has been viewed an amazing two million times on YouTube, reports The Sun.

It led scientists to discover that parrots – and also elephants – do feel the beat of music, giving them an in-built sense of rhythm for dancing.

But researchers found no evidence that cats, dogs or chimps shared this trait.

Dr Aniruddh Patel, of the Neurosciences Institute in San Diego, California, said scientists began their research after becoming mesmerised by the footage of Snowball.

He said: 'I was very impressed and contacted Snowball's owner in Indiana for a more formal test. This showed that Snowball wasn't just mimicking the movements of somebody off-camera.

'And his movements followed the beat of his favourite Backstreet Boys song even when the tune was sped up or slowed down.'

Dr Patel said Snowball drifted in and out of following the beat – 'like a child does'.

But he added that statistical analysis of the cockatoo's head bobs showed they really were related to tempo.

And after analysing 1,000 videos purporting to show animals dancing, the scientists found 14 species of parrot and one species of elephant that they say were convincing dancers.

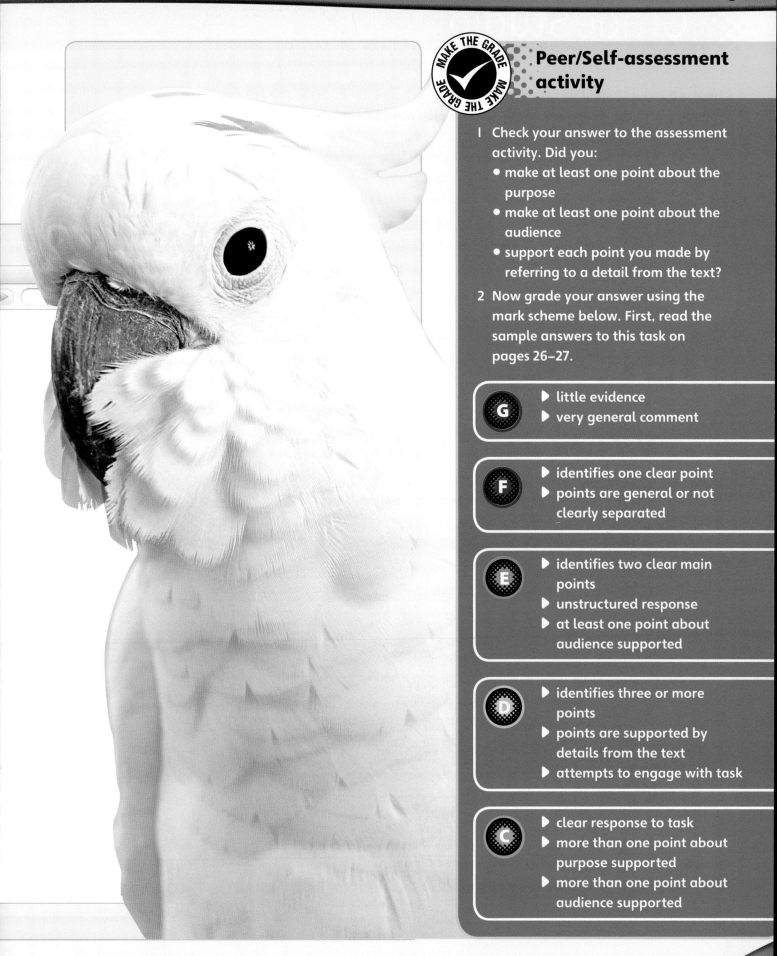

Peer/Self-assessment activity

MAKE THE GRADE · MAKE THE GRADE

1 Check your answer to the assessment activity. Did you:
- make at least one point about the purpose
- make at least one point about the audience
- support each point you made by referring to a detail from the text?

2 Now grade your answer using the mark scheme below. First, read the sample answers to this task on pages 26–27.

G
- little evidence
- very general comment

F
- identifies one clear point
- points are general or not clearly separated

E
- identifies two clear main points
- unstructured response
- at least one point about audience supported

D
- identifies three or more points
- points are supported by details from the text
- attempts to engage with task

C
- clear response to task
- more than one point about purpose supported
- more than one point about audience supported

Here are three student answers to the activity on pages 24–25. Read the answers together with the examiner comments, and then complete the final peer/self-assessment task.

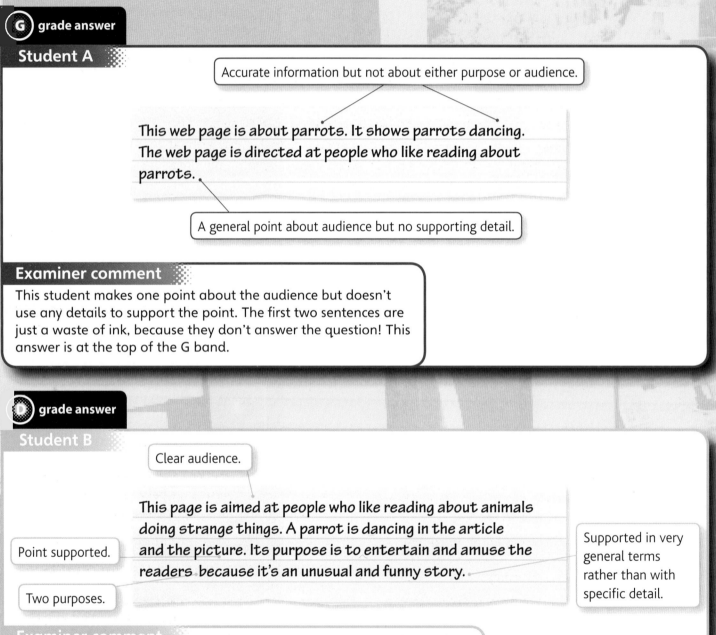

G grade answer

Student A

Accurate information but not about either purpose or audience.

> This web page is about parrots. It shows parrots dancing. The web page is directed at people who like reading about parrots.

A general point about audience but no supporting detail.

Examiner comment

This student makes one point about the audience but doesn't use any details to support the point. The first two sentences are just a waste of ink, because they don't answer the question! This answer is at the top of the G band.

D grade answer

Student B

Clear audience.

Point supported.

Two purposes.

> This page is aimed at people who like reading about animals doing strange things. A parrot is dancing in the article and the picture. Its purpose is to entertain and amuse the readers because it's an unusual and funny story.

Supported in very general terms rather than with specific detail.

Examiner comment

There is one clear audience here and two purposes, but the supporting detail is mixed: the audience is clearly supported but the points about purpose need more precise detail. This is in the D band.

Student C

Purpose – to inform.

Supported.

Audience.

Supported.

More support for the same point.

Audience.

Audience.

Supported.

The purpose is to inform about some research done on parrots dancing; the scientist, Dr Patel, is quoted. It is also intended to amuse people who like funny stories. It is funny to find parrots dancing and the story was published in the 'quirky' category – meaning a strange and funny story. It may appeal to people who like to spend a lot of time on the internet, because it is from a website. It might also appeal to animal lovers because it is about a parrot.

Examiner comment

This is a full and detailed answer, with each point supported by a detail from the text. It makes several points about purpose and several about audience, and therefore is right at the top of the C band.

 MOVING UP THE GRADES

Purpose and audience

To move up the grades, you need to make sure that everything you write is focused directly and clearly on the task. The more different points you can make, the better. Each point you make should be supported by a detail in the text.

Student A makes three points but only one of them is relevant to the task.

Student B's answer is better because it makes more than one relevant point and gives a little supporting detail.

Student C's answer is by far the best because it makes several clear points about both audience and purpose and then supports them.

Putting it into practice

Explain what you now know about:

- finding points to make about purpose
- finding points to make about audience
- answering the question
- finding precise support for the points you make
- what makes the difference between an G, D and C answer on purpose and audience.

In the future:

- practise finding purpose and audience with any text you come across
- you could practise with newspapers, magazines, pages from textbooks, letters and advertisements
- practise finding precise details to support the points you make
- for each type of text, give yourself about 10 minutes to practise this skill.

What are arguments?

An **argument** is what the text has to say. It is the point that the writer is trying to make. When you are trying to work out the argument of a text, try the following:

- look at the headline first – there may be a clue
- try to work out what the main point of the article is.

What are facts?

A **fact** is something that can be proved to be true. The most obvious facts are names and places and dates and figures. This is because these can be looked up and checked. For example, the sentences below are facts:

- London is the capital of England.
- The Olympics will be held in London in 2012.

When you are trying to find facts:

- Don't read the whole article first – skim it.
- First, look for names of places or people (with capital letters).
- Then look for numbers or dates.

What are opinions?

An **opinion** is what someone thinks. Opinions are different from facts because opinions cannot be proved to be true. For example:

- London is the greatest city in the world.
- London was by far the best choice for the Olympics.

When you are looking for opinions in a text:

- Don't read the whole article first – skim it.
- Look for quotations (in quotation marks) first.
- Then read the article to find other opinions – especially those of the writer.

The text below shows some examples of argument, fact and opinion.

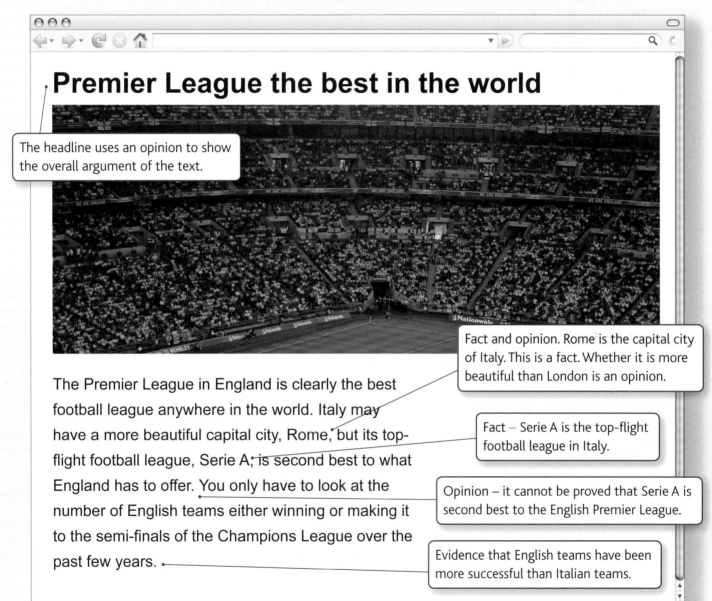

Premier League the best in the world

The headline uses an opinion to show the overall argument of the text.

Fact and opinion. Rome is the capital city of Italy. This is a fact. Whether it is more beautiful than London is an opinion.

The Premier League in England is clearly the best football league anywhere in the world. Italy may have a more beautiful capital city, Rome, but its top-flight football league, Serie A, is second best to what England has to offer. You only have to look at the number of English teams either winning or making it to the semi-finals of the Champions League over the past few years.

Fact – Serie A is the top-flight football league in Italy.

Opinion – it cannot be proved that Serie A is second best to the English Premier League.

Evidence that English teams have been more successful than Italian teams.

Activity 1

1   Look at the 'Heaven on Earth' article opposite.

2   First, try to work out what the main argument of this text is. Is the writer saying that Salento is a nice or an unpleasant place to visit? A good way of doing this is to look at the headline first – this often gives a clue.

3   Now find and write down **four** facts from this article. Once you have found four facts stop reading. Remember: a fact is something that can be proved to be true.

4   Next, find and write down **three** opinions given in the article. Once you have found three opinions stop reading. Remember: an opinion is what someone thinks. An opinion cannot be proved to be true.

Facts used	Opinions used
1 _____	1 _____
2 _____	2 _____
3 _____	3 _____
4 _____	

Check your answer

In your answer to Activity 1:

When looking for four facts:
- Did you skim the article first?
- Did you look for names of places or people (with capital letters)?
- Did you look for numbers or dates?

When looking for three opinions:
- Did you skim the article first?
- Did you look for quotations?
- Did you read the article to find other opinions?

The Sunday Telegraph

HEAVEN ON EARTH

SALENTO, ITALY

WHO Writer Charlie Higson

WHY 'Because it's so far off the beaten track'

I love Salento, in Apulia, in the southernmost part of Italy's 'heel', because it's relatively undiscovered – at least by British visitors – and very different to the rest of Italy. They say it's like Tuscany was 30 years ago before we Brits descended on the place and, in the act of discovering it, spoilt what it was we had discovered.

It's very flat and not in any way picturesque, unlike so much of Italy, but the Italians go there in their droves for six weeks in the summer. The rest of the year it's empty, so if you go then, you can really get away from it all.

The people are still fiercely independent from the rest of Italy and Salento is a lot more wild and rugged than the northern part of Apulia, but that's part of the attraction. It's also home to Lecce, which has been called the 'baroque capital of southern Europe'. It's the sort of treasure that makes you think 'why have I never heard of this place?' I guess the answer is simply because it's off the beaten track, even though it used to be a fixture on the Grand Tour.

There's a wonderful hotel called the Masseria Montelauro (0039 0836 806203; www.masseriamontelauro.it) in Otranto. A masseria is the name for the North African-style farmhouses that dot the area, some of which have been turned into hotels.

And the food in Salento, especially the seafood, is fantastic.
There are lots of little family-run restaurants in the region, most of which are excellent.

I'm particularly partial to La Locanda (0039 0832 603519) in Carpignano, where they serve the catch of the day. Despite being in a village, it's busy year round, a recommendation in itself.

I'd urge you to discover Salento while it's still 'undiscovered', so to speak. The spring, when wild flowers swathe the hillsides, or the autumn, are both wonderful times to visit.

Charlie Higson is author of the 'Young Bond' series of children's novels. Details at www.youngbond.com.

Step back in time: part of the Roman theatre in Lecce, 'the baroque capital of southern Europe'

Your learning

This lesson will help you to:

- find the main points in an argument
- follow an argument
- select material to answer the question.

Re-cap: what is an argument?

An argument is what the text has to say – the point it is making. A writer may make one or more points to support an argument. In the next activity you will look at a text and identify the different points a writer makes.

Remember, when you are trying to work out the argument of a text:

- always look at the headline first – there may be a clue

- try to work out what the main point of the article is

- think about how the writer moves from one point to another during the course of the argument.

Activity 1

1 Read the 'Heaven on Earth' article on page 31 again. The main argument of this text is that Salento is an attractive place to visit.

2 List the main points the writer makes to persuade the reader that Salento is an attractive place to visit.

Before you do this, look at the following tips:

- Make sure you are clear on what the main argument of the text is.

- Now read the text. Each time you come across a different point that supports the argument, underline it.

- Make sure you read right to the end of the text so that you cover all of the points.

- Write each point down in a list. For example:

1 The writer says Salento is a good place to visit because it is relatively undiscovered by tourists.

2

3

Activity 2

Now you need to put everything that you have done in this and the previous lesson together. You have already been asked to identify facts and opinions and the different points a writer makes to support the argument. This activity asks you how facts and opinions are used to support the argument in the 'Heaven on Earth' text.

Each time you come across a main point ask yourself these questions:
- Does a fact support what the writer says?
- If so, which one?
- Does an opinion support what he has to say?
- If so, what opinion is it?

Asking yourself these questions will make sure that each time you mention a point you show how it is supported by a fact or by an opinion.

Now answer the following question.

How does the writer use facts and opinions to support his argument in the article 'Heaven on Earth'?

You could write your answer like this:

The writer's argument is that Salento is a beautiful place to visit. He uses numerous facts to support his argument, for example, _____ _____ . He also uses opinions, such as _____ and _____ .

Check your answer

In your answer to Activity I:
- Did you find several points that support the main argument?
- Did you list them clearly?

Activity 3

1. Read the article 'Mothers worth £33,000 a year'.

2. Make some notes on the following.
   - What work in the house do mothers and fathers do?
   - What is said about childcare?
   - What is said about insurance?
   - What are the pressures on parents?

3. Now answer the following question.

What are the main points made in the article and how are they supported?

Mothers worth £33,000 a year

By Sarah O'Grady, Social Affairs Correspondent

MOTHERS do nearly £33,000 worth of jobs around the house free of charge every year – 40 per cent more than fathers, research showed yesterday.

Women spend an average of 74 hours a week on household chores and childcare, tasks that it would cost £32,812 to pay someone else to do, according to insurer Legal & General.

By contrast, men spend only 53 hours a week on domestic tasks, although it would still cost £23,296 to pay someone to do everything that fathers do for free.

Within these totals, women spend 33 hours a week looking after children, 50 per cent more than the 21½ hours men spend with their offspring each week. Full-time mothers put in the most work around the house, carrying out an average of 82 hours worth of jobs each week, while women who work full-time fit in 55 hours of chores and childcare on a weekly basis.

Daily Express

The insurer said the value of work carried out by mothers in a year had increased by more than £8,000 since it last conducted the research in 2005.

Alan Ferguson, protection marketing and channel development director at Legal and General, said: 'Mums are a rock for many families, making sure that the home runs smoothly, that the children are looked after and often holding down a job of their own.'

But despite the high value of the tasks carried out by mothers, only 53 per cent have life insurance and just 26 per cent have critical illness cover.

Instead, 35 per cent of parents questioned said they would rely on grandparents to help look after children if one of them died, while 30 per cent said they would work part-time.

Just over half of people said they would make cutbacks if one parent was unable to work due to an accident or illness and 38 per cent would rely on their partner's wage, while 37 per cent said they would get sick pay. Three-quarters of working mothers said they felt under pressure to work to help pay the bills, although 52 per cent said they did not just work for the money.

Only 17 per cent of people pay someone to help out around the house, despite 27 per cent saying cleaning and tidying up is the job they least like doing, while 25 per cent dislike doing the washing and ironing and 15 per cent hate gardening.

Marketing consultants Bdifferent questioned 1,000 parents during January.

Check your answer

GradeStudio

In your answer to Activity 3:
- Did you mention housework?
- Did you mention childcare?
- Did you mention insurance?
- Did you mention how parents would cope if they were ill?
- Did you mention how the main points are supported by facts?

Activity 1

1. Read the article by Carole Malone about Jade Goody, which was written shortly before she died.

2. Now take 10 minutes to answer the following question.

   What are the main points Carole Malone makes to support her argument that it is 'Time to turn the cameras off Jade'?

Time to turn the cameras off Jade

IS IT just me who's starting to feel like the spectre at the feast? Am I the only one feeling grubby, ashamed and just a little bit sickened at watching a young woman die in front of my eyes?

Am I the only person looking at pictures of Jade Goody where her face is contorted with pain, when she's gasping for breath through an oxygen mask, where she stares through car windows with sad, dead eyes – and thinking **ENOUGH!**

Jade Goody has always been upfront about her reasons for allowing the cameras to film the various stages of her illness. She was always clear she was doing it so her sons would have enough money for the kind of life she never had. But that was before she knew she was going to die.

That was when she still knew her own mind.

Coping

And I was part of that deal. I interviewed her – twice. And I was proud of what we did. I was proud of how, together, we got what she wanted to say across to people who, till then, were suspicious about her motives for living and coping with this disease so publicly.

But when I spent time with Jade she could still talk. She could still think for herself. She still had hope. She was still in control of what was happening to her.

And even when the doctors delivered her death sentence – on one of the very days I was interviewing her – even then she still had the strength to organise the wedding she had always dreamed of.

Back then – and incredibly it was only three weeks ago – Jade was in control of everything down to the caterers she wanted, the dress she wanted, her bridesmaids. She even set about organising a helicopter to take her to the ceremony.

But now she's not in control. Now, what's left of her life revolves around numbing the pain which often has her screaming in agony. And when she's not begging doctors to get her out of the pain, she's flailing around in a drug-induced stupor – not knowing where she is or what she's doing.

NEWS OF THE WORLD

And we're all watching that. We're all part of this gruesome peep show that's charting this young woman's final, agonising days. We're all staring wide-eyed through a window **SHE** opened not wanting to look – but not being able to resist.

Max Clifford said last week: 'Jade will tell us when she's had enough.'

Will she? How will she do that when she's slurring, semi-conscious and up to her eyeballs on morphine?

How's she going to tell the photographers waiting outside the hospital to go away when she needs every ounce of strength just to breathe and stay alive? How's she going to make them understand that being photographed in her nightie looking sick and distressed isn't how she wants people to see her?

And **I KNOW** she doesn't want people seeing her like that because when, just over a month ago, we took photos after she first lost her hair she was insistent on wearing beautiful clothes and having her make-up done.

'I might have cancer but I don't want to look like I have,' she told me. 'I still want to look pretty.'

But she doesn't look pretty any more. She looks sick. But most of all she looks hunted – like an animal.

And it's frightening. Not just for all those people who presently have cancer who look at Jade and know what their end is going to be like. But it's terrifying for the rest of us who, for now at least, don't have cancer but see Jade as a hellish glimpse of what might be waiting for us down the years.

Macabre

The wedding should have been the cut-off point. Those photos of her in her wedding dress looking serene and beautiful – **THAT'S** the moment we should have bid Jade a dignified farewell.

THAT'S how we should have remembered her – happy, smiling, looking into the eyes of the man she adores and holding hands with the sons she will never see grow up.

Because what we're seeing now is macabre and dark. And it's gratuitous. I don't want to see Jade's last breath. I don't want to see her struggling to stay alive so her sons can be christened. I don't want to see her straining to give a thumbs-up sign to the cameras to make **US** feel better.

This is now a horror show – the only difference is that it's real.

Jade has lived her whole adult life in front of the cameras. But it's time now to turn them off. We've seen enough. She's shared enough.

Her final days belong to her – not us.

Peer/Self-assessment activity

1 Check your answer to the assessment activity. Did you:
   - manage to find several different points
   - manage to present these clearly
   - manage to make everything you wrote relevant to the question
   - manage to avoid repeating the same point?

2 Now grade your answer using the mark scheme below. First, read the sample answers to this task on pages 38–39.

G
▸ some writing about the text
▸ some relevant material

F
▸ identification of one clear point
▸ mainly copying
▸ points general or not clearly separated

E
▸ identification of two clear main points
▸ unstructured response

D
▸ identification of three or more points
▸ attempts to answer the question

C
▸ clear and effective attempt to answer the question
▸ range of relevant points
▸ material chosen to focus on reasons for turning cameras off

Here are three student answers to the activity on pages 36–37. Read the answers together with the examiner comments, and then complete the final peer/self-assessment task.

F grade answer

Student A

Accurate information but not tied to question.

The writer thinks it's a bit sick watching Jade Goody. She was strong enough to arrange her wedding but she is now in pain. She looks ill and it's frightening.

Needs more careful angling to question.

Reason.

Reason.

Examiner comment

Some of this information could be angled more successfully to answering the question. The student needs to use the key words of the task in order to make the points completely relevant. This answer is at the bottom of the F band.

E grade answer

Student B

The writer thinks it's bad to watch someone who was healthy and in control of her life but who is now sick and dying. She doesn't look as good as she used to do and she has been in front of the cameras for long enough.

Clear point.

Reason.

Reason but not explained.

Examiner comment

This answer covers some of the main points and is clear, but it's brief and only covers a small part of what is in the article. It is in the E band.

Student C

Reason.

Reason.

Clear reason.

Before she was about to die, Jade Goody liked being in front of the cameras but now she is dying it is unpleasant to watch. Previously she was in control of her life but now she is not. She is drugged with morphine and doesn't know what she is doing a lot of the time. She wouldn't want people to see her looking bad because she always wanted to wear make-up and nice clothes. It is frightening to see her dying. The cameras should be turned off because then she could have been remembered the way she wanted to be.

Clear reason.

Supported.

Clear reason.

Clear reason.

Examiner comment

This is a clear answer with several points and clear explanations about why the cameras should be turned off. All the comments are made relevant to the task. It is in the C band.

MOVING UP THE GRADES

Argument, fact and opinion

Read the question you have to answer before you read the passage. When you are reading the text, underline the key points so that when you have finished you just have to focus on these to write your answer.

If you are asked to find facts and opinions, try to find the most obvious ones.

If you are showing the different points in an argument, make sure that you don't repeat yourself.

Putting it into practice

Explain what you now know about:

- finding facts
- finding opinions
- following an argument
- finding the main points in an argument
- answering the question.

In the future:

- you can practise this skill with any text you come across
- take a few minutes to find some facts
- take a few minutes to find some opinions
- work out what is the main point being made
- find the different points that make up the argument.

Implications and assumptions

Your learning

This lesson will help you to:

- understand the implications of what is written
- understand the assumptions that the writer makes about the readers.

What are implications?

An **implication** is something that is suggested rather than said directly. For example, if you say 'He's not short of a penny or two', you are implying that he is well off. Or when the boxer Muhammed Ali described himself as being able to 'Float like a butterfly and sting like a bee', he was implying that he was light on his feet and could punch hard.

What is an assumption?

An **assumption** is when something is taken for granted. Writers often make assumptions about their readers – perhaps what the reader knows about or how old the reader is. For example, a football article does not explain who managers and players are because the writer assumes that the readers already know this.

Activity 1

In this activity, you need to work out the implied meaning of a statement.

1 Look at the following statement.

> 'When John thinks, he can do some good work.'
> This **implies** that most of the time John doesn't think.

2 Now read each of the statements below and say what the implied meaning is.

> **a** Margaret's handwriting is much neater than it used to be.
> **b** The Minister has decided to spend more time with his family.
> **c** This washing powder is cheaper than some other leading brands.
> **d** It won't take as long as you think.

Activity 2

1 Read the following text from a TV magazine.

The 40,000-year-old baby!

Baby Mammoth: Frozen In Time
SUN 8pm NATIONAL GEOGRAPHIC Documentary

A baby mammoth found frozen in the Arctic ice has rocked the scientific world!

Two years ago, in the Siberian Arctic, a reindeer herder made an astonishing discovery. It was the body of an extinct baby woolly mammoth from the Ice Age – 40,000 years ago!

Yuri Khudi's amazing find caused great excitement among scientists and sparked a remarkable adventure, with tests carried out by boffins in Russia and all over the globe.

new!

Yuri (second right) watches scientists work on his find

This one-off film follows the little mammoth's discovery and uses computer graphics to recreate her life in the Ice Age.

Named Lyuba – which means 'love' in Russian – after Yuri's wife, the baby mammoth was near-perfectly preserved after being trapped in permafrost for thousands of years. Experts were able to analyse every aspect of her body with scans and biopsies – and even discover how she lost her life.

Researchers estimate that she was barely a month old and probably died from suffocation after becoming trapped in mud.

But Lyuba's death wasn't in vain, as scientists hope she will help them solve the bigger mystery of why all mammoths eventually died out.

Words by Anne Richardson

2 Answer these questions to work out the purpose of the article and the writer's assumptions about the reader.

a What is the article advertising?

b What is the picture for?

c What kind of magazine is the article from?

d Who might be reading this article?

3 Now answer the following question.

What does the writer of the article assume about the readers' interests? Use details from the text to support your points.

Make sure that you support each of the points you make by referring to something specific in the text.

Check your answer

GradeStudio

In your answer to Activity 2:
● Did you answer each of the questions?
● Did you give a piece of evidence from the text for each point you made?

Reading between the lines

Your learning

This lesson will help you to:

- think about the implications of what is written
- think about the assumptions that the writer makes about the readers
- select material to answer questions about implications and assumptions.

Re-cap

In the last lesson, you started to look at the assumptions that a writer makes in a text. In this lesson, you will also try to read between the lines to work out the implied meaning of a text.

Activity 1

This activity asks you to look at some of the assumptions that are made about who might be reading an article and what they know.

It also asks you why you think the verse was included at the end. This is to see if you can work out what is implied at the end of the article.

I Read the leader article from the *Sun* opposite.

2 Answer the following questions.

    a What does the article assume the reader knows about?

    b What is its main purpose?

    c How serious do you think the article is?

    For each of your answers, use some evidence from the text.

3 Now look at the verse in this text.

    a Why do you think it has been included?

    b Why has the line '… Your job is safe, Carol' been added after the verse? What does this imply about:

- how good an example of poetry this is
- how good a poet Carol Ann Duffy is?

Thanks, Carol

WE promise it won't go to our heads, but new Poet Laureate Carol Ann Duffy praises Sun headlines as a source of laughter and inspiration.

We're delighted Carol appreciates Britain's favourite paper. And as we might say…

> *We try to make life bright and sunny,*
> *For 30p – that ain't much money.*
> *News and sport, jokes and fun,*
> *Never be without your Number One Sun.*

…Your job is safe, Carol.

Sun

Reading between the lines

Now you need to look in detail at the assumptions that are made about the audience for a text. This includes things like:

- who they are
- what they like
- what they dislike
- how old they are.

Activity 2

I Read the following advertisement.

'The dancers are young and sexy, the repertoire is new and the dancing is always superlative.'

The Times

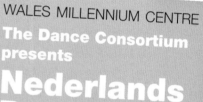

WALES MILLENNIUM CENTRE

The Dance Consortium presents

Nederlands Dans Theater 2

19 & 20 Jun '09

Fri & Sat 7.30pm, Tickets £10, £14, £18, £24

£28 SuperSeat includes best available seat, free programme & exclusive use of bar pre-show & interval.

With their unique brand of energy and vivacity, Nederlands Dans Theater 2 (NDT2) have become firm favourites with British audiences.

The commitment of these extraordinary young dancers is so strong that as well as working and dancing together, they also choose to live together collectively, sharing a house in the middle of Den Haag, where they are based. This directly adds to the strength of their partner work; you will be hard pushed to find a group of dancers more physically or mentally in tune with one another.

With none of the dancers older than 23, age means nothing to virtuoso skill and technique, as they revel in flaunting their superb talent on stage, spreading an infectious energy among audiences that complements this exceptional technical ability. These are the very best young dancers from around the world – hundreds audition but only a few are chosen.

NDT2 presents three pieces by Lukáš Timulak, Ohad Naharin and Jiří Kylián.

wmc.org.uk

2 For each of the following questions, write at least one sentence and try to include evidence from the text.

   a What activity does the advert assume the reader will be interested in?

The activity assumes the reader is interested in

_____

because the article is about _____ .

   b Look at the quotation from *The Times*. What has the writer assumed about the readers' ages?

The quotation from *The Times* shows that the writer thinks the readers are _____
because the quote mentions _____ .

   c How does the picture support this idea?

   d How does the language in the main text support the assumption that the audience will be attracted by the youth and energy of the dancers?

Check your answer

In your answer to Activity 2:
- Did you answer all the questions?
- Did you use evidence from the text to support your answer?

Assessment practice

This lesson will help you to:

- practise an exam-style question
- assess your answer by comparing it with what other students have written.

Activity 1

1 Read the article from the *News of the World*.

2 Now take 10 minutes to answer the following question.

What assumptions does the article make about its readers, and what is the article really about?

In order to do this, you should think about each of the following questions.

1 What TV programme does it expect the reader to know about?

2 Which people are the readers supposed to recognise?

3 What one piece of information is given about Rachel Riley, and why?

4 What point about politics is the article making?

3 For each answer, give a detail from the text to support your idea.

NEWS OF THE WORLD

We've got it figured

REPORTS that *Countdown*'s Rachel Riley's maths aren't up to predecessor Carol Vorderman's standard may not equal disaster.

After all, if Oxford graduate Rachel fails her sums on the Channel 4 show she can always try the Treasury.

Where the numbers seldom add up.

Peer/Self-assessment activity

1 Check your answer to the assessment activity. Did you:
- answer each question
- answer them in the order they appeared
- give a piece of evidence from the text to support each point you made
- make sure that you had used the sub-questions to answer the main question?

2 Now grade your answer using the mark scheme below. First, read the sample answers to this task on pages 48–49.

G
▶ some writing about the text
▶ some relevant material

F
▶ identification of one clear point
▶ points general or not clearly expressed

E
▶ identification of two clear main points
▶ unstructured response

D
▶ identification of three or more points
▶ attempts to answer the question

C
▶ clear and effective attempt to answer the question
▶ range of relevant points
▶ material chosen to focus on assumptions about readers and what article is really about

Here are three student answers to the activity on pages 46–47. Read the answers together with the examiner comments, and then complete the final peer/self-assessment task.

Student A

Accurate information but doesn't answer the question.

It does, but what does this show about what the article is really about? Answer not made clear.

> This is a short article from the *News of the World*. It is about Rachel Riley and Carol Vorderman who are TV presenters. It is about what happened in 'Countdown'. It mentions the Treasury at the end.

Accurate information but not angled to the question, though it might have been written to show what it is assumed the reader knows.

Examiner comment

This student has chosen material which could have been angled to answer the question, but it wasn't. The student just gives information from the text without answering the question directly. There are hints of what the assumptions about the readers are and a hint of what the main purpose might be, but the answer is too indirect to respond to the task properly. The answer is in the F band.

Student B

Assumption.

Assumption.

> This article expects the readers to know what 'Countdown' is and who Rachel Riley and Carol Vorderman are. It tells us that 'Countdown' is on Channel 4 and implies that the programme has something to do with maths. It implies that Rachel Riley is clever because it says she is an Oxford graduate.

Implication.

Supported.

Implication.

Examiner comment

This makes two clear points about assumptions, although it doesn't really support them. It makes two points about implications and supports one of them. It doesn't mention what the article is really about and so only answers part of the question. It is therefore in the D band.

Student C

Assumption.

Assumption.

Supported.

Implication.

Supported.

Supported.

Supports following point.

Details of implication.

Implication.

Details of implication.

This programme assumes that the readers know about TV because it mentions a Channel 4 programme, 'Countdown'. It also assumes they know who Carol Vorderman and Rachel Riley are, suggesting that they are involved with the programme. It tells us that the programme has something to do with maths because it talks about Rachel Riley doing her sums. But the article isn't really about 'Countdown'. It is about politics. It attacks the Treasury and implies in the last sentence that the government doesn't know what it's doing.

Examiner comment

This is a full and detailed answer which answers both parts of the question in detail and supports each of its points by reference to a detail the text. It is at the top of the C band. You don't, of course, have to know anything about 'Countdown' itself to answer the question fully.

Implications and assumptions

To move up the grades you need to make a wider range of points and answer all of the question.

You can also go up the grades by making sure that you support all your points with references to specific details in the text.

This is clearly shown in the difference between the answers from Student A (who barely answers the question and provides no supporting details), Student B (who answers half the question with some details) and Student C (who answers all of the question with good supporting details).

Putting it into practice

Explain what you now know about:
- finding assumptions in a text
- finding implications in a text
- supporting your points by reference to the text's details
- what makes the difference between an F answer, a D one and a C one.

In the future:

- you can practise this skill with several of the texts you come across
- ask yourself:
  - what the text assumes the reader knows
  - what it doesn't assume the reader knows
  - what it implies about something rather than directly stating it
- for each type of text, give yourself 10 minutes to practise this skill.

Language features

Your learning

This lesson will help you to:

- identify and name language features
- comment on the effect of language features.

Getting started with language

You already know a great deal about language because you have been studying it since you started school. In the exam, though, students often panic and forget about some of the basic things they know, such as the following.

What is a noun?	Nouns are names of things, e.g. book, page, table, chair.
What is a verb?	Verbs are 'doing' words, e.g. read, run, sleep, jump.
What is an adjective?	Adjectives are words that describe nouns, e.g. bright, green, beautiful.
What is an adverb?	Adverbs are words that describe verbs, e.g. quickly, slowly.

Activity 1

When answering a question about language features, the first step is to identify the language feature and to give an example of it.

1 Read the short text about a Cornish pasty competition.

2 Now find and write down:
- three nouns
- three adjectives
- three verbs
- two adverbs.

If you are unsure, check your words against the definitions at the top of the page.

'We were conned,' said Cornish pasty man

A Devon pasty maker was given the prize last week for the best Cornish pasty in Britain. The organizer said that there had been an administrative mistake because the rules ought to have stated that entrants had to come from Cornwall, but this had unfortunately been missed off the information given to entrants.

The managing director of the winning firm Chunk thought that it was a case of sour grapes on the part of the Cornish entrants. 'It seems the Cornish may have got a bit podgy round the waist when it comes to pasty-making and have been relaxing and rather resting on their laurels,' he said. He thought his firm's tasty pasty definitely deserved to win.

In the exam you might be asked to find some language features and comment on their effect.

Activity 2

Look again at the text opposite and your answers to Activity I. Choose one noun, one adjective, one verb and one adverb and make a comment about the effect of each of them.

Here is one to begin with:

> The writer uses the adverb 'unfortunately' to make the reader aware that an unlucky mistake was the cause of the misunderstanding.

Check your answer

GradeStudio

In your answer to Activity 2:
● Did you identify the four language features?
● Did you comment on the effect of each of them?

The effect of language features

Your learning

This lesson will help you to:

- identify and name language features
- comment on the effect of language features.

Re-cap

In the last lesson you looked at some of the basic features of language, such as the use of nouns, verbs, adjectives and adverbs.

You will no doubt have looked at lots of other language features. Here is a list of some other language features you might be familiar with:

Feature	Example
First person	I, we
Second person	you
Third person	he, she, it, they
Metaphor	the room is a prison
Simile	the room is like a prison
Repetition	location, location, location
Rhyme	soar, roar
Slang	bling
Puns	the footballer kitted his kitchen out
Alliteration	grimy green gunk

Activity 1

1. Now read the article opposite called 'Plod with the bod'. It uses lots of language features to try and make the reader interested in reading the article.

2. Try to find **five** different language features and label them. Then, for each one:
   - name the feature
   - write down the example
   - make a comment about how the feature interests the reader.

   You can do all three things in the same sentence, For example:

Names the feature.

Gives the example.

Makes the comment.

The article starts with alliteration ('Meet man mountain') to make it sound catchy from the beginning.

Sun

PC GARY IS STRONG ARM OF THE LAW

PLOD WITH THE BOD

By JOHN TROUP

Copper's a whopper ... Gary Rogers in uniform and in bodybuilder's pose

MEET **man mountain Gary Rogers … the copper known as PC BOD.**

Bodybuilder Gary, 45, stands 6ft 3 ins, weighs 19st, has incredible 21ins biceps and thinks nothing of pushing 200kg weights.

He has collared thousands of crooks during 22 years as a PC – and admits his rippling muscles are a huge help when tackling troublemakers.

Dad-of-three Gary said: 'I get a lot of people saying they wouldn't want to mess with me.

'Occasionally idiots want to try it on, but usually my physical presence helps calm situations.'

Police colleague Anne-Marie Bullivant said: 'We always feel safer with Gary around, but he's a gentle giant.'

Gary, who serves with the Met in Barnet, North London, used to be a powerlifter who represented the force in competitions.

He switched to bodybuilding six years ago after injuring both knees, and last month won his regional heat in the national Stars of Tomorrow contest.

His daily fitness regime involves getting up at 4am to pump iron for three hours, and he eats a strictly-controlled high protein diet.

Gary, from Leighton Buzzard, Beds, added: 'When I go into schools it's handy to be able to talk about things like fitness, and not just about crime. If I can help get young people into sports, that can only be a good thing.'

j.troup@the-sun,co.uk

Grammar features and their effects

In the exam, you might also be asked to comment on grammar.
There are four basic kinds of sentence that are frequently used.

▶ **Simple sentence**

This is a sentence (usually a short one) with a subject and a main verb. |For example:

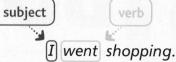

I *went* shopping.

▶ **Compound sentence**

This is a series of two or more simple sentences joined together (usually with the conjunctions 'and' or 'but'). For example:

conjunction

I went shopping and bought Bill a birthday present but I then decided to have lunch.

▶ **Complex sentence**

This is a longer sentence with one or more parts that depend on the main part (joined to it using what is called a subordinating conjunction such as 'although', because', 'until'). For example:

subordinating conjunction

I went shopping because I needed to buy Bill a birthday present.

▶ **Minor sentence**

This is a sentence which breaks the rules of grammar because it doesn't have a verb in it! These are often used for dramatic effect, to provide contrast to what has gone before or to jolt the reader. For example:

Gutted!

You can also identify and comment on particular kinds of sentences, such as questions, exclamations, rhetorical questions and any sentences that have grammar which breaks the rules or make a deliberate grammatical mistake.

Activity 1

Look at the seven sentences below. For each one, write down whether it is a simple, compound, complex or minor sentence. Look at the definitions opposite to remind you of the different types of sentences.

1 I went straight home and did my homework.
2 I went straight home.
3 I went straight home because I had lots of homework to do.
4 Home at last!
5 My mother was at home because she also had some work to do.
6 I met my friends in front of the Town Hall in the evening before we all went to the cinema.
7 I went home and wrapped Gemma's present.

Grammar features and their effects

In the exam, you will also need to comment on the effect of grammar choices. Look at this piece from a website about places to visit. The notes show you how to make a comment on the sorts of sentences being used and their effect.

http://www.organge.co.uk/travel/holidayideas

Eccentric Britain – quirky days out

The follies of Mad Jack

John 'Mad Jack' Fuller was the undisputed king of folly building. Not for him a lone concrete monument. Instead, he built a remarkable number of note-worthy temples, needles and towers – just for the fun of it. He constructed his tomb in the shape of a pyramid and a temple in the grounds of his estate.

Not content with that, he added an obelisk (to commemorate the Battle of Waterloo) and a sugar loaf cone, supposedly to win a bet. But he wasn't done yet. After adding an observatory, he built a tower at the site in Brightling, completely hollow and serving no useful purpose: the very definition of a folly.

Where is it? Around Brightling, East Sussex. Get **driving directions**.

When can you go? Any time of the year.

How much? Free of charge.

Find out more on the **Folly Towers** website.

> Simple sentence to grab the reader's attention and to introduce the topic.

> Minor sentence (without a verb) to make it sound dramatic.

> Unusual grammar (beginning the sentence with 'But' in order to make the story dramatic and make the reader want to find out what came next).

> Simple questions.

> Minor sentences (without verbs) in order to make the answers punchy.

The writer uses a variety of different kinds of sentences to make the writing varied and get the reader interested in the story.

Activity 2

Read the article below, taken from the internet.

The definitive guide to the ugliest cars ever

`http://orange.co.uk//cars`

R925 BDV

Dax Kamala

One car that will never be described as cute as a Koala is the Dax Kamala (we do poetry too, you know).

Looking more like a duck-billed platypus than the ultimate sports performance car, it seems some crazy person out there won't give up the dream that this hideous car could go big, with it making an appearance at the British International Motor Show in 2008 (it's true, we saw it with our own eyes). A bit odd, as it is said to have gone out of production because of a lack of popularity. We wonder why?

It really underlines just how bad the Kamala is that, despite its impressive performance capabilities of 0–60 mph in 3.9 seconds and a top speed of 160 mph, only 30 units of this special, special car that first appeared in 1996 were made before it was sold onto Kamala by Dax in 2001. Not something that will go down as the business decision of the century. And if its looks weren't hilarious enough, apparently Kamala means 'terrible' in Finnish. Enough said.

Now answer the following question.

How does the writer use language and sentence structures to make the article interesting to the reader?

First, identify the feature you want to talk about. Then think about the effect it has. Finally, write this up as a sentence, for example:

'The article finishes with the minor sentence "Enough said".
This emphasises in a humorous way that there is simply nothing else to say about this ridiculous car.'

Your learning

This lesson will help you to:

- practise an exam-style question
- assess your answer by looking at other responses.

Activity 1

1. Read the text 'It's a purr-fect crime'.

2. Identify and label any language and grammar features you can find. Look back at pages 50–57 if you need a reminder of these features.

3. Answer the question below.
   How are language and grammar features used in this article, and what are their effects?

   Write your answer in the following way.
   - Name the feature.
   - Give an example from the text.
   - Comment on its effect on the reader.

   You can do all three things in one sentence. Write as many sentences as you can, covering both language and grammar features in 15 minutes.

It's a purr-fect crime

CAT STEALS ODD SOCKS

BY ROD CHAYTOR
rchaytor@mirror.co.uk

FOR weeks Henry the cat has been leading a secret life of crime … nicking neighbours' socks then stashing them under his bed.

The serial cat burglar would regularly select them from nearby washing lines, until shocked owner Louise Brandon, 40, caught him bang to rights.

Louise said: 'He jumped over the back fence as bold as brass with a black sock hanging from his mouth. He froze, then walked past me into the house.

'When I followed him, I saw he'd built up a pile of socks behind his bed in the kitchen. There were 51 different socks of all shapes and sizes.'

Daily Mirror

FELINE GUILTY Henry

Mum-of-one Louise has now asked her neighbours in Loughborough, Leics, if they are missing any, but she has so far failed to reunite any missing pairs.

She said: 'It's embarrassing. I've got a bag full of other people's socks.'

And pussyfooting one-year-old Henry shows no sign of kicking his sock habit.

'We took the socks away but he just goes out and steals more,' said Louise.

Baffled expert Sally Walker, of the Woodside Animal Centre in nearby Braunstone Frith, Leicester, said: 'Cats like to bring gifts home – usually birds or mice – but never socks.'

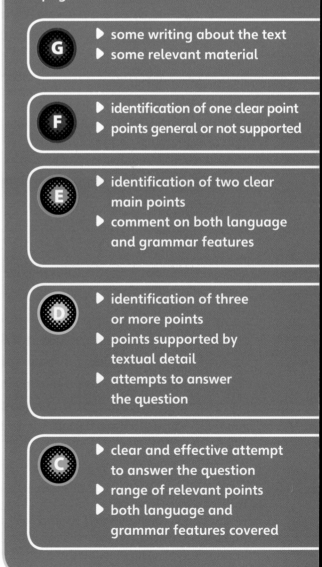

Peer/Self-assessment activity

1 Check your answer to the assessment activity. Did you:
 • identify several language features
 • comment on the effect of the language features
 • identify several grammar features
 • comment on the effect of the grammar features?

2 Now grade your answer using the mark scheme below. First, read the sample answers to this task on pages 60–61.

G
 ▶ some writing about the text
 ▶ some relevant material

F
 ▶ identification of one clear point
 ▶ points general or not supported

E
 ▶ identification of two clear main points
 ▶ comment on both language and grammar features

D
 ▶ identification of three or more points
 ▶ points supported by textual detail
 ▶ attempts to answer the question

C
 ▶ clear and effective attempt to answer the question
 ▶ range of relevant points
 ▶ both language and grammar features covered

Here are three student answers to the activity on pages 58–59. Read the answers together with the examiner comments, and then complete the final peer/self-assessment task.

Student A

Information not made relevant to task.

This mentions presentational devices, not the language and grammar features that were asked for.

Detail of language feature.

This text is about Henry the cat who has been leading a secret life by stealing the neighbours' socks and putting them under his bed. The cat's owner is Louise Brandon. There are two headlines – one at the top of the page and the second in the middle in capital letters. The main headline is a joke. It makes a pun on the cat (which purrs) and the crime which is perfect. This makes the reader laugh.

Language.

Clear comment on effect.

Examiner comment

Most of the answer is irrelevant to the task. However, towards the end it names one language feature (pun) and makes a clear comment about it. There is nothing on grammar. It only answers part of the question and is in the F band.

Student B

Language feature.

Comment on effect.

Language feature.

Comment on effect.

Supported.

There is a pun in the headline to amuse the reader. Because the story is about a cat that steals socks, the crime is described as 'purr-fect' because cats purr. The story also uses slang ('nicking' and 'stashing') to make the story seem funny. There are quite a lot of simple sentences such as 'It's embarrassing' in order to make it easy for the reader to read.

Supported.

Supported.

Grammar feature.

Comment on effect.

Examiner comment

There are two clear supported examples of language, each with a comment on effect. There is one supported comment on grammar with a comment on effect. It fulfils all the grade D descriptors and is at the top of the D band. It's a shame there aren't more points.

Student C

Language feature.

Comment on effect.

Supported by detail.

Language feature.

Supported by detail.

Language feature.

Supported by detail.

Grammar feature.

The headline's pun amuses the reader because the cat thief's crime is described as 'purr-fect' rather than 'perfect'. The slang word 'nicking' is used to make the cat sound like a criminal by using language usually related to criminals. Personification is also used to amuse the reader as the cat is described as 'selecting' the socks to steal. The direct speech is mainly simple sentences such as 'It's embarrassing' because the cat belongs to ordinary people. There are some complex sentences ('When I followed him') but these are not complicated because the writer wants the reader to follow the story easily.

Comment on effect.

Supported by detail.

Comment on effect.

Comment on effect.

Comment on effect.

Supported by detail.

Grammar feature.

Examiner comment

This is an effective answer that is to the point. Each time a feature is named, the student gives an example and makes a comment. The answer covers both language and grammar. It is well into the C band.

MOVING UP THE GRADES

Language and grammar features

Make sure that you look at the question carefully to see if you are being asked about language features, grammar or both.

For each feature that you mention, name the feature, give an example and make a comment.

This will keep you on track throughout your answer and the more of these you can do in the time allowed (which will be about 10 minutes), the better.

Putting it into practice

Explain what you now know about:
- finding language features
- commenting on language features
- finding grammar features
- commenting on grammar features
- answering the question.

In the future:

- you can practise these skills with any text you come across
- take a few minutes to identify some language features
- take a few minutes to identify some grammar features
- practise writing sentences where you name the feature, give an example and make a comment.

Your learning

This lesson will help you to:

- identify and name presentational features.

Presentation

Any text you read has an author who has written the words and decided how the text is going to look – the presentation.

If you have some text you can do different things to change the way it looks. You will be used to doing this on a computer, using the menus or toolbar.

There are a lot of different presentational features that you can use:

- size of font
- type of font
- graphics (photos, diagrams, drawings, graphs, logos etc.)
- colour
- headings
- spacing of the text.

Alongside is a text where the designers have done a lot to make it look interesting. Look at the annotations and think about the effect of each of these choices on the reader.

SUNDERLAND

Ricky hopes there's no repeat

RICKY SBRAGIA asked for his old job back after witnessing the debacle of Sunderland's last trip to Everton.

The Scot, who was last night made permanent manager at the Stadium of Light following a successful spell as caretaker boss, returns to Goodison Park this afternoon hoping history does not repeat itself.

Sbragia was sat in the stands on November 24 last year after accepting Roy Keane's offer of employment on Wearside.

Sunderland were trounced 7-1, leaving Sbragia worrying whether he had made the right move in leaving Bolton and he decided to contact Wanderers boss Gary Megson.

Sbragia said with a smile: 'I was sitting up in the stand wondering what was happening.

'I was thinking about not joining Sunderland after that, to be honest with you.'

'I actually sent a message back to Gary Megson asking if the job was still available.

'He said, "You have got some defending to do," and that was it.

'We were too open as a team that day. We conceded four goals right down the middle, so defensively we were poor.

> Opening paragraph in bold and name in bold capitals to grab reader's interest.

> Direct speech in bold italics to highlight dramatic statement.

Sbragia in the hotseat

THE PEOPLE

Finger goes over into white space to make him seem dynamic as if his arm is moving.

Headline in large capitals to make it stand out.

BY JAMES **COURAGE**

'We were depressed because it was a hammering. To be fair, it could have been more.

'But we could have scored a couple – it could have ended up maybe 12-3 on the day. That was the first time I joined Sunderland, so it would be nice to go back there and get something from the game.'

Now, 13 months or so on, Sbragia goes back to the blue side of Merseyside, to face a resurgent Everton who moved up to sixth place with a 1-0 Boxing Day success at Middlesbrough.

And maybe it is the memory of that thumping defeat, rather than Friday's 0-0 draw at home to Blackburn, that is influencing his thoughts on whether to play one or both of his strikers, Djibril Cisse and Kenwyne Jones, today.

He said: 'It is a problem – it's the main problem: who do we play up front?

'Djibril likes to play on his own – Kenwyne can do that, but Djibril gives us a little bit extra, he gives us that pace over the top.

'On the one hand, we want them to play together and get some sort of continuity, but you are also going into the game thinking about possibly dropping one.

But there's a reason for that. We have got to make a decision about how we go.'

FACT FILE
Born 26 May 1956, Lennoxtown, Scotland.

PLAYING CAREER
Defender 1974–85, at Birmingham, Greenock Morton, Walsall, Blackpool, York and Darlington.

COACHING CAREER
Began at York in 1987. Moved to Man Utd in 2002 as reserve team boss. Joined Bolton in October 2005 as first team coach. Sunderland first team coach in November 2007 then caretaker manager on Dec 4 this year when Roy Keane quit.

Fact file in different type for those who perhaps don't want to read all the article.

Activity 1

1 Read the text opposite, which was used for an advertisement.

2 Create a finished version of this text by using different presentational features to make it look like an advertisement. Try to make it look interesting to read.

3 Remember to think about the following when creating your new text:
- size of font
- type of font
- graphics (pictures, graphs, logos etc.)
- colour
- headings
- spacing of the text.

Check your answer

GradeStudio

In your answer to Activity I, did you use:
- spacing
- different fonts
- different sizes of print
- headings
- colour
- pictures?

They both lower cholesterol.

Which would you rather have?

Thankfully, one daily bottle of Benecol Yogurt Drink is twice as effective at reducing your cholesterol than eating approximately three bowls of oats a day.

That's because only Benecol contains unique plant stanols, which are scientifically proven to reduce your cholesterol. No other food is more effective.

So enjoy Benecol every day as part of a healthy diet and lifestyle. For more information visit benecol.co.uk

Take control of your cholesterol

The facts: One bottle of Benecol Yogurt Drink contains 2g of plant stanols, which reduces LDL cholesterol by up to 14% when consumed daily.

Daily consumption of approximately three bowls (90g) of oats contains 3g beta-glucan which reduces LDL cholesterol by up to 5%.

Your learning
This lesson will help you to:

- identify and name presentational features.

Re-cap

In the last lesson you made decisions about how to present some text. In this lesson you will compare your choices to those made by the professionals! You will also start to find and name presentational features in texts.

Activity 1

Opposite is what the advertisers did with the text from Activity I on pages 64–65. They will probably have made some different decisions from those you made. They may have thought about things you didn't think about. The idea is to try to make a dull text look interesting.

1 Look at the text:

2 Find an example of each of these presentational features in the text.
- headings
- colour
- bold text
- different sizes of print
- logo
- pictures.

Check your answer

GradeStudio

In your answer to Activity I:
Did you find examples of all six presentational features listed above?

They both lower cholesterol. Which would you rather have?

Thankfully, one daily bottle of Benecol Yogurt Drink is **twice as effective** at reducing your cholesterol than eating approximately three bowls of oats a day.

That's because only Benecol contains unique plant stanols, which are scientifically proven to reduce your cholesterol. No other food is more effective.

So enjoy Benecol every day as part of a healthy diet and lifestyle. For more information visit benecol.co.uk

Benecol®

Take control of your cholesterol

The facts: One bottle of Benecol Yogurt Drink contains 2g of plant stanols, which reduces LDL cholesterol by up to 14% when consumed daily. Daily consumption of approximately 3 bowls (90g) of oats contains 3g beta-glucan which reduces LDL cholesterol by up to 5%.

Activity 2

1 Read the article below. It is taken from the *Sun* newspaper.

2 Find as many presentational features as you can.

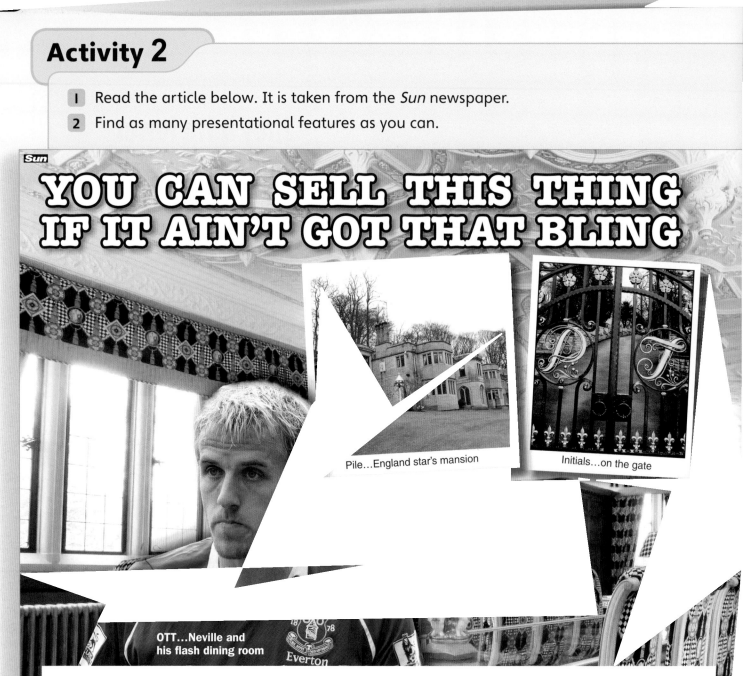

Sun

YOU CAN SELL THIS THING IF IT AIN'T GOT THAT BLING

Pile...England star's mansion

Initials...on the gate

OTT...Neville and his flash dining room

Neville must axe 'gaudy' fittings to flog home

By BEN ASHFORD

England soccer ace Phil Neville has been told to tone down his 'gaudy' mansion if he wants to sell it.

The Everton captain and wife Julie kitted out their dining room and bedroom in favourite WAG label Versace.

The proud pair also plastered their initials P and J on the front gates and carpets.

But Neville, 31, has had to slash £600,000 off the £4million price of the sprawling six-bedroom home in Crawshawbooth, Lancs, after failing to find a buyer in seven months.

Phil Spencer, presenter of Channel 4 property show *Location, Location, Location*, said: 'Anyone buying a home that gaudy and personalised would almost be obliged to change it.

'After paying that amount of money they will want to do their own thing. And it's a difficult time to sell.'

Check your answer

Now check your answer to Activity 2 against the list of presentational features below. If you missed any, label them now.

- headline
- capital letters
- picture
- italic font
- inset pictures
- captions
- underlining
- bold font

In the exam, you might be asked to comment on the effect of some of these presentational features.

For example, here are some comments on the effect of the presentational features in the 'You can sell this thing if it ain't got that bling' article.

The picture of Phil Neville lets the reader know what he looks like.

The picture of the room supports the view that the fittings are 'gaudy'.

Activity 3

Look at your answer to Activity 2. Take **three** of the presentational features that you have found and make a comment about their effect. Number your features: 1, 2, 3.

Commenting on presentational features

Activity 1

1. Look closely at the 'Screech Owl Sanctuary' text opposite.

2. Find examples of the presentational features that the designer has used. Here is a list to help you:
   - heading
   - capital letters
   - cartoon-style graphics
   - pictures
   - round inset
   - different print sizes
   - italics
   - different colours
   - curved banner.

3. Choose **four** of the presentational features in your list. For each of your chosen features, write one sentence about how it makes the owl sanctuary seem an attractive place to visit.

Structural features

In the exam, you might also be asked about structural features of a text. Here are some commonly used structural features:

- paragraphs, stanzas, bullet points, sections
- introduction, conclusion, summary, repetition
- words that help to structure a text, such as 'first', 'secondly', 'in conclusion'.

Activity 1

Look at the way this text from a food page is structured into sections.

Instructions to use scissors to cut it out for a recipe book

Bold heading in a bigger font to make the recipe clear

dinner tonight   **Lindsey Bareham**

Chunky vegetable soup with pesto

Finely chop the onion. Heat the oil in a medium-sized pan, add the onions and a generous pinch of salt, cover and cook over a gentle heat for 5 minutes. Peel the carrots, swede and potato and dice into Dolly Mixture-sized pieces. Rinse, drain and stir into the onions. Cover and cook for 5 more minutes, stirring once, then add the stock. Increase the heat and bring to the boil, adjust the heat and simmer for 10–15 minutes until the vegetables are tender. Shred the cabbage or chard, rinse and shake dry. Immerse it in the soup to cook for a few minutes until just tender. Taste the broth and adjust the seasoning. Serve with a dollop of pesto, a swirl of your best olive oil, plenty of grated Parmesan and brushcetta. For the brushcetta, toast the bread, rub one side with garlic and dribble with olive oil.

Serves 2.
Prep: 15 min.
Cook: 30 min.

I medium onion, approx 75g
1 tbsp olive oil
2 carrots
150g swede
1 potato, approx 150g
600ml chicken stock (cube is fine)
150g cabbage or chard
2 tbsp pesto
1 garlic
3–4 tbsp best olive oil
Freshly grated Parmesan, to serve
2 slices sourdough bread

Coloured picture to make the page look more attractive

Three sections with a heading over the writing

Instructions in a block in the middle

Ingredients in list form

Activity 2

Look at the text below. Now answer the following questions to help you understand how structural features are used.

1 Why do you think the headline runs right across the article?

2 How many sections is the article in?

3 How are the different sections separated out?

METRO

Transport for London

METRO TRAVEL

DLR to benefit from massive 2012 Games investment

The Docklands Light Railway (DLR) will benefit from £80million in improvements to prepare the network for the 2012 Olympic and Paralympic Games.

The enhancements will help boost annual passenger numbers from 67million to 100million by 2012. The improvements are funded by the Olympic Delivery Authority (ODA) and are outlined in its new publication, 'pace'.

The investment will contribute to schemes that expand the network, increase the number of rail cars and provide an even more reliable and frequent service. Passengers will benefit as early as 2010, when the first projects will be completed.

Four new stations – Star Lane, Abbey Road, Stratford High Street and Stratford International – will be built along the Stratford international extension, which will open in July 2010. These will give people who live in the area a better and more frequent connection to the Olympic Park and other London 2012 venues served by the DLR. They will also support the community, which has suffered from poor access to transport.

Director of the DLR, Jonathan Fox, said: 'DLR is already ahead of the game in its plans for 2012 thanks to funding and support from the ODA. The extensions and upgrades we will have in place will not only make for a successful Olympic and Paralympic Games but provide reliable and well-connected public transport for years to come.'

■ *The ODA document can be downloaded from www.london2012.com/publications*

Did you know?

- Around 500,000 people are expected to use the DLR on each day during the first week of the 2012 Games
- On average, 18,600 people use the DLR to Stratford Regional station every day but this will increase to 75,000 during the games
- There will be 27 DLR trains per hour on the Stratford International extension into the heart of the Olympic Park, in games time, and there will be a 25 per cent increase in the length of the DLR by 2010
- All DLR stations are step-free, there is level access between the floor of the train and platforms, and carriages are spacious, benefiting wheelchair users and passengers with mobility aids

Check your answer

GradeStudio

Look at the annotated copy of the DLR article below. Does your answer to the questions in Activity 2 on page 73 include the points made below?

Article headline running right across the article to link the three sections.

Main story in two columns.

Overall: spacing, colour, font size, underlining, different-coloured bullets and bold headline used to separate out different elements in the article.

Transport for London

METRO**TRAVEL**

DLR to benefit from massive 2012 Games investment

The Docklands Light Railway (DLR) will benefit from £80million in improvements to prepare the network for the 2012 Olympic and Paralympic Games.

The enhancements will help boost annual passenger numbers from 67million to 100million by 2012. The improvements are funded by the Olympic Delivery Authority (ODA) and are outlined in its new publication, 'pace'.

The investment will contribute to schemes that expand the network, increase the number of rail cars and provide an even more reliable and frequent service. Passengers will benefit as early as 2010, when the first projects will be completed.

Four new stations – Star Lane, Abbey Road, Stratford High Street and Stratford International – will be built along the Stratford international extension, which will open in July 2010. These will give people who live in the area a better and more frequent connection to the Olympic Park and other London 2012 venues served by the DLR. They will also support the community, which has suffered from poor access to transport.

Director of the DLR, Jonathan Fox, said: 'DLR is already ahead of the game in its plans for 2012 thanks to funding and support from the ODA. The extensions and upgrades we will have in place will not only make for a successful Olympic and Paralympic Games but provide reliable and well-connected public transport for years to come.'

■ *The ODA document can be downloaded from www.london2012.com/publications*

Did you know?

• Around 500,000 people are expected to use the DLR on each day during the first week of the 2012 Games

• On average, 18,600 people use the DLR to Stratford Regional station every day but this will increase to 75,000 during the games

• There will be 27 DLR trains per hour on the Stratford International extension into the heart of the Olympic Park, in games time, and there will be a 25 per cent increase in the length of the DLR by 2010

• All DLR stations are step-free, there is level access between the floor of the train and platforms, and carriages are spacious, benefiting wheelchair users and passengers with mobility aids

Four sections (separate introductory paragraph, main news story, picture, Did you know? box).

Activity 3

Label each of the following structural and presentational features in the text below.

picture	headline	sub-headings	underlining
bold print	box	different sizes of print	bullet points
groups of three	conclusion	introductory paragraph	

Still Alive and Kicking

A great survivor

Although William Shakespeare was born in Stratford-on-Avon in 1564, his work is very much alive and well in the twenty-first century. He's the only writer whose work every school pupil studies and one of the most popular dramatists of all time. His work can be seen regularly on the stage today. The Royal Shakespeare Company keeps his work alive in his home town and recently showed every single one of his plays in one season in Stratford.

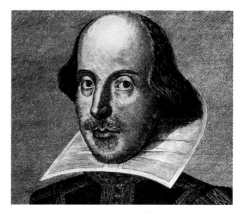

A man of his time

Shakespeare didn't shy away from topics which were controversial and which interested and worried his contemporaries. His plays dealt with political prisoners, political murders, rape, incest, homosexuality, class and gender identity, racism, Jewish persecution, religion, arranged marriages, exploitation – to name but a few of his subjects.

A man for our time

The closest modern equivalents of Shakespeare's plays are TV soap operas. They, too, deal with up-to-date contemporary issues. They, too, make their stars into celebrities. They, too, made pots of money for their production companies, as Shakespeare's plays did for the companies he wrote for.

A man for all time

Like no one else, Shakespeare wrote about issues which affect all people, regardless of their particular culture or the particular time they live in. If you want to know about these, then look no further than Shakespeare's plays:

• Love	• Politics	• Government
• Friendship	• Relationships	• Gender
• Sexuality	• Identity	• Religion
• Prejudice	• Crime	• Punishment

Your learning

This lesson will help you to:

- practise an exam-style question
- assess your answer by comparing it with what other students have written.

Activity 1

1. Look at the 'Eden Project' text and label **six** presentational and structural features. Look back over pages 62–75 if you need a reminder of the different presentational and structural features.

2. Choose **four** features from your list whose effect you feel you can comment on.

   Now answer the question below.

   How are presentational and structural features used in this charity leaflet, and what are their effects?

   Write your answer in the following way.

   - Name the feature.
   - Give an example from the text.
   - Comment on its effect on the reader.

   You can do all three things in one sentence. Write as many sentences as you can, covering both presentational and structural features in 15 minutes.

http://www.edenproject.com

Some facts

When we were young the playground began at our front gates, but children today aren't going out to play because 'it's dirty, it's wet' and they're spending less and less time together.

Sounds trivial?

- By 2010 one in five of our children will be clinically obese.
- The government says that a lack of play is as damaging as junk food for children.
- Our children are suffering from depression and are being treated with anti-depressants.
- One in ten children today has a mental-health problem.

The Eden Trust is a registered Charity no.1093070
The Eden Project, Bodelva, St Austell, Cornwall PL24 2SG
Tel. +44 (0)1726 811911 **Fax.** +44 (0)1726 811912
www.edenproject.com

www.edenproject.com

How you can help

Mud Between Your Toes runs courses for primary and secondary school children and for young people from disadvantaged backgrounds.

They help to develop self esteem, confidence, social and thinking skills in participants and raise environmental awareness.

Some of the activities include:

- Survival skills
- Orienteering
- Cooking
- Shelter building
- Craft skills

By supporting us today you can help us get children back outside to re-connect them with the natural world.

Below are some examples of what your money could do each month.

£5 could pay for an Explorer Pack including quiz and information sheets, magnifying glass, compass, map, pencil and notebook.

£10 could pay for a survival skills kit including waterproofs, whistle, map, compass, torch, food, matches, pocket knife and first aid kit.

£15 for a teacher, artist or expert to work with a class of children for one day (based on a total cost of £180).

All donations go to **Mud Between Your Toes**. For more information go to www.edenproject.com/what-we-do/mud-between-your-toes

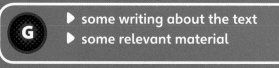

Peer/Self-assessment activity

1   Check your answer to the assessment activity. Did you:
- identify structural features
- comment on the effect of the structural features
- identify presentational features
- comment on the effect of the presentational features?

2   Now grade your answer using the mark scheme below. First, read the sample answers to this task on pages 78–79.

G
▶ some writing about the text
▶ some relevant material

F
▶ identification of one point
▶ some attempt to comment

E
▶ identification of two clear main points
▶ comment on both structural and presentational features
▶ some extra material

D
▶ identification of three or more points
▶ some detail in support of answer
▶ attempts to answer the question

C
▶ clear and effective attempt to answer the question
▶ range of relevant points
▶ both structural and presentational features covered

Here are three student answers to the activity on pages 76–77. Read the answers together with the examiner comments, and then complete the final peer/self-assessment task.

F grade answer

Student A

Presentational feature.

Presentational feature.

> This advertisement has some facts about children and some pictures showing children outside. It prints what you have to pay in bold letters. and gives an email address in large print.

Not made relevant to task.

Detail from text to support.

Presentational feature.

Examiner comment

The response names three presentational features but only gives supporting detail for one of them. It doesn't make any comments on effect. It only answers part of the question and is in the F band.

D grade answer

Student B

Supported by detail.

Comment on effect.

Supported.

Comment on effect.

Supported.

Structural feature.

> The text is broken up into sections, using paragraphs and bullet points. It uses colourful pictures to show children being active and make the reader want to support the charity. It highlights in bold what different amounts of money could buy in order to make the reader want to donate money. It gives the email address in large bold print.

Presentational feature.

Presentational feature.

Examiner comment

This starts by mentioning structure but doesn't comment on effect. There are then two comments on presentational features, both supported by reference to the text's details and both with a comment about effect. The last sentence forgets to mention the effect. There is some identification of main points here, but not all the points are completely successful. The answer is in the D band.

Student C

Presentational feature.

Structural feature.

Presentational feature.

Supported.

Supported.

Presentational feature.

The leaflet is structured by using headings such as 'Some facts', one-sentence paragraphs, like the first one and bullet points as in the 'Sounds trivial' section. This makes it easy to read, a bit at a time. The headings are in bold to make it eye-catching and the colour pictures of children involved in activities make the reader think the project is worthwhile.

Comment on effect.

Examiner comment

This is a concise and effective answer which each time names the feature, gives an example and makes a comment. It covers both structure and presentation. Although many more points could have been made, it is well into the C band.

MOVING UP THE GRADES

Presentational and structural features

Make sure that you look at the question carefully to see if you are being asked about presentational features, structure or both.

For each feature that you mention, name the feature, give an example and make a comment.

This will keep you on track throughout your answer and the more of these you can do in the time allowed (which will be about 10 minutes), the better.

Putting it into practice

Explain what you now know about:
- finding presentational features
- commenting on presentational features
- finding structural features
- commenting on structural features
- answering the question.

In the future:

- you can practise these skills with any text you come across
- take a few minutes to identify some presentational features
- take a few minutes to identify some structural features
- practise writing sentences where you name the feature, give an example and make a comment.

Your learning

This lesson will help you to:

- compare texts
- select material to answer the question.

Compare

In the exam, you are likely to be asked to compare texts. This means finding **similarities** and **differences** between texts – for example, how they are presented, their language, their purpose and audience.

Activity 1

Look at the two information texts opposite and answer the following question.

Compare the ways in which information is presented in these two texts.

Follow the steps below.

1 Read the question carefully. Make a note of the key words in the question – *ways*, *information*, *presented*.

2 Make a list in two columns of the methods used to present information. Some ideas are listed below to get you started.

Text A	Text B
colour	colour
heading	numbers and key

3 Now look at your table and think about how you are going to compare the texts. You could:

- write about all the similarities first, then the differences
- write about all the differences first, then the similarities
- take each method in turn and compare the similarities and differences.

Whichever you do, try to find several different things to compare.

4 Now write your answer, making sure that you are comparing methods. You could start your answer like this:

Both texts use colour, but whereas Text A uses _____ , Text B uses _____ . These colours are chosen because _____ .

Text A

THE TIMES

dinner tonight

Lindsey Bareham

Rosemary lamb with haricot beans

Smear the steaks with olive oil. Finely chop the onion and garlic. Heat the remaining oil in a medium, heavy-bottomed pan and stir in the onion, garlic and rosemary with ½ tsp salt. Cover and cook over a low heat for 10–15 minutes, until the onion is limp and slippery but hardly coloured. Chop the anchovies and stir into the onions with the tomato paste and wine or water. Rinse the beans and stir into the onions. Season with salt and pepper and simmer for 10 minutes. Heat a grill pan or heavy frying pan. When very hot, season one side of the steaks and cook, seasoned side down, for 2–3 minutes, depending on the thickness. Turn and repeat seasoning and cooking. Rest on a chopping board for 5 minutes, then slice across the grain into chunky strips. Pile lamb and juices over the beans (rosemary discarded).

Serves 2–3
Prep: 15 mins
Cook: 20 mins
2 lamb rump steaks, approx
    250g in total
2 tbsp olive oil
2 onions, approx 75g each
1 garlic clove
3 sprigs rosemary
2 anchovy fillets or 1 tsp
    anchovy paste
1 tbsp tomato paste
150ml white wine or water
400g can haricot beans
½ lemon

Text B

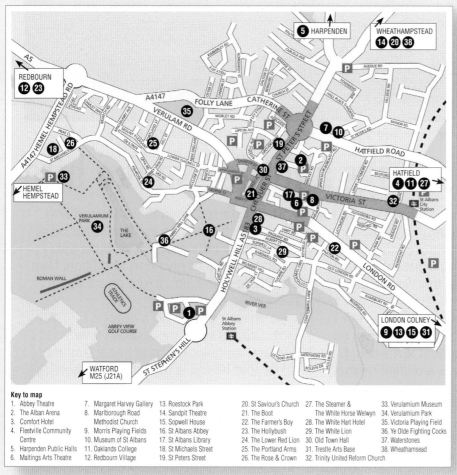

Key to map

1. Abbey Theatre
2. The Alban Arena
3. Comfort Hotel
4. Fleetville Community
   Centre
5. Harpenden Public Halls
6. Maltings Arts Theatre

7. Margaret Harvey Gallery
8. Marlborough Road
   Methodist Church
9. Morris Playing Fields
10. Museum of St Albans
11. Oaklands College
12. Redbourn Village

13. Roestock Park
14. Sandpit Theatre
15. Sopwell House
16. St Albans Abbey
17. St Albans Library
18. St Michaels Street
19. St Peters Street

20. St Saviour's Church
21. The Boot
22. The Farmer's Boy
23. The Hollybush
24. The Lower Red Lion
25. The Portland Arms
26. The Rose & Crown

27. The Steamer &
    The White Horse Welwyn
28. The White Hart Hotel
29. The White Lion
30. Old Town Hall
31. Trestle Arts Base
32. Trinity United Reform Church

33. Verulamium Museum
34. Verulamium Park
35. Victoria Playing Field
36. Ye Olde Fighting Cocks
37. Waterstones
38. Wheathamsead

Activity 2

Something else you might be asked to compare is language and/or the purpose of two texts.

1 Read the texts below (from the *Daily Express* newspaper) and opposite (from FirstGroup plc website).

Daily Express

LOSS OF BLOOD: O'Grady 'in recovery mode' with Dannii Minogue and Al Murray

Paul says fangs a lot for snake bite

CHAT-SHOW host **Paul O'Grady** showed no signs of permanent trauma following his snake bite scare as he partied with showbiz pals **Dannii Minogue** and comedian **Al Murray** at this week's English National Ballet bash.

The former Lily Savage comic was left in fear for his life after a 4ft adder bit him on the arm at his home in Kent last week, but by Thursday night it was a distant memory.

'I saw the snake lying on the wood pile and shooed it away with a broom. I didn't know it had bitten me until I saw two puncture marks,' O'Grady, 53, recalled.

'Then I started pouring with blood and bled badly for four hours. That is because I am already on a drug which thins the blood because of my heart condition. I am like Carrie in the film, it just pours out of every orifice.'

He doesn't even hold a grudge.

'You can't blame the snake, I love snakes,' he quipped, 'and I hear that the adder that bit me is now on a drip getting life support, poor thing.'

your station
at King's Cross

The massive £400 million redevelopment of King's Cross station means changes for First Capital Connect customers in the near future.

In the coming weeks and months Network Rail will be:

- Closing the First Capital Connect ticket office outside platforms 9–11 and moving it to platform 8.
- Starting structural alterations to the front of First Capital Connect platforms 9–11.
- Moving the toilets and left luggage office on platform 8 to the main concourse.
- Closing Marks & Spencer and other shops along platform 8.

New hoardings mean it may take you a minute or two longer to leave platforms 10 and 11 during the rush hour. The new temporary toilets, however, will have level access instead of the steps you currently have to negotiate.

By 2012 the entire station will be transformed, giving First Capital Connect passengers arriving at platforms 9–11 direct access to a new concourse with three times the existing space and links to a new London Underground ticket office below.

2 Follow the steps below to help answer the following question.

Compare the ways in which the texts use language to fulfil their purposes.

I Complete the table below to say what each text is for.

Text A	Text B
To inform about a TV star	To inform about changes to King's Cross station

2 Complete the table below with examples of language features from each text.

Slang – bash	Use of lists
Direct quotations	Formal language – *negotiate*

3 Make a note of details in the texts that show how the language features are used to fulfil the purpose in each case.

4 Write your answer.

Check your answer

GradeStudio

In your answer to Activity 2:

- Did you find any differences in the purposes of the two texts?
- Did you find any similarities in the purposes of the two texts?
- Did you find language features to compare?
- Did you support your points by using details from the text?

Your learning

This lesson will help you to:

- collate information
- compare texts.

What does 'collate' mean?

'**Collate**' means 'put together'. In the exam, if the question asks you to collate, you might have to choose material from several texts and then answer a task based on what you have chosen.

Activity 1

Read the newspaper headlines below, then answer the following question.

How do the writers and designers of three of these headlines try to make the readers want to read the articles?

You are given five headlines, but are only asked to write about three, so you need to:

- look closely at all five headlines
- decide which three you could say most about
- try to find at least two things to say about each of the three you have chosen.

Remember: the question doesn't ask you to compare the headlines.

1

PHIL THE CRACKS!
<u>Players turning on Scolari</u>

2

Bring back the beaver – he will save money and clean our rivers

3

I CANUTE BELIEVE IT, MY HOME IS SAVED

4

Vince swims against the sea of sewage

5

Bother from Brussels Bureauprats

Activity 2

This activity looks at the same headlines you have just written about. However, this time it is a **compare** question.

1 Remind yourself of the headlines and the advice above, then answer the following question.

Compare the ways in which the writers and designers of three of these headlines try to make the readers want to read the articles.

Here is some advice to help you to tackle this question.
- Choose three headlines that you have something to say about.
- Take each headline in turn and make a list of all the ways it interests the reader.
- Compare your lists for each of the three headlines. What similarities and differences can you see?
- Remember, you only need to compare two headlines at a time.

2 Now write your answer. You could write your answer in the following way.

Both Headline 2 and Headline 4 use alliteration [give examples] in order to [make comment about effect].

Check your answer

GradeStudio

In your answer to Activity 2:
- Did you make a comparison in each sentence?
- Did you find several similarities?
- Did you find several differences?
- Did you make your points clear to the reader?

Your learning
This lesson will help you to:
- practise an exam-style question
- assess your answer by comparing it with what other students have written.

Activity 1

This activity asks you to compare two accounts of the same story. The accounts are about the same event and appeared in different newspapers on the same day. Read the texts (opposite and on pages 88–89) and then answer the following question.

Compare the ways this story is presented. Write about:
- **the information**
- **the headlines**
- **the language**
- **the presentational devices.**

Sun

It's a plant, officer
DRUG RAID OVER SMELLY FLOWERS

High jinx ... top, where plant grew, below, front door, and left, Ivor in garage

By JOHN COLES

DRUG squad cops raided an elderly couple because a plant in their garden smelled like CANNABIS.

Shocked Ivor and Margaret Wiltshire returned from holiday to find their front door kicked in and their house and garage searched.

The police left empty-handed because the tell-tale smell was caused by a tiny creeping flower called Moss Phlox.

It was the **SECOND** time the pongy plant had been mistaken for pot.

Four days before the police raid, the Wiltshire's neighbours David and Christine Difford were terrified when a gang wearing Hallowe'en masks turned up demanding drugs.

David, 54, said: 'They shouted, "Give us the weed, man" and searched the loft. It was frightening.'

Retired engineer Ivor, 77, dug up the Phlox and has received an apology from police, who said the raid followed 'other investigations'.

Ivor, who has no sense of smell, said in Kingswood, Bristol: 'We can't believe such a small plant has caused so much trouble.'

Daily Mirror

Dopes!

OAPS RAIDED FOR GROWING PLANT THAT SMELLS LIKE POT

BY GEOFFREY LAKEMAN

POLICE smashed down the front door of an OAP couple to swoop on their 'cannabis' horde – a sweet-smelling £2 plant bought from the garden centre.

Ivor and Margaret Wiltshire, 77 and 79, bought the moss phlox four years ago but it was only this summer that the pink plant gave off a pungent aroma similar to cannabis.

And the smell was so strong their next-door neighbours were even threatened by a drug gang who broke in and demanded: 'Give us the weed.' And weeks later Ivor and Margaret came home from holiday in October to find the door battered down and the drug squad inside. The grandfather-of-three, who has had no sense of smell since an operation 30 years ago, said: 'It multiplied fast. I was happy because it looked so nice.

'I haven't got any idea what cannabis smells like and certainly never smoked it.

'I was so distressed that I felt like digging up the whole garden. We can't believe such a small plant has caused so much trouble.'

The couple even noticed a police helicopter hovering in Kingswood, Bristol – now thought to have been using infrared to find the heat source of the cannabis 'factory'.

And neighbours David and Christine Difford, 54 and 56, said of the terrifying raid by a masked gang: 'They were very keen to look in the loft which left me baffled. But I'm not surprised at the police raid. You could smell it all the way up the road.' Avon and Somerset police, which is investigating, said: 'We received a complaint and have apologised.'

> **I've no idea what cannabis smells like. I've certainly never smoked it**
>
> **IVOR WILTSHIRE**

WRONG
MOSS PHLOX

RIGHT
CANNABIS

Peer/Self-assessment activity

1 Check your answer to the assessment activity. Did you:
   - cover all four bullet points
   - find some similarities
   - find some differences?
2 Now grade your answer using the mark scheme below. First, read the sample answers to this task on pages 90–91.

G
▶ some writing about two texts
▶ some attempt to compare

F
▶ identification of one clear point
▶ an attempt to compare

E
▶ identification of at least two clear points
▶ some comparison
▶ deals with at least two bullets

D
▶ some identification of main points
▶ comment on at least three bullets
▶ some comparison
▶ attempts to answer question

C
▶ clear and effective attempt to answer question
▶ range of relevant points
▶ all four bullets covered
▶ range of comparisons

Here are three student answers to the activity on pages 86–89. Read the answers together with the examiner comments, and then complete the final peer/self-assessment task.

F grade answer

Student A

Some information but very general.

Too vague for any clear comparison.

True, but this was given in the question.

Both stories are about some old people and them growing plants in their gardens. They cover the same basic information. Both texts have headlines and both have pictures to make the reader interested in the story.

A very general comparison.

A general comment.

Examiner comment

This answer covers some very basic general information but there is no supporting detail and there is only material about one bullet which was not given in the task itself. It is just into the F band.

D grade answer

Student B

Vague opening sentence not yet answering the question.

Although both stories are the same, there are some differences. The ages of four people are given in the *Daily Mirror* but only of two in the *Sun*. The *Mirror's* headline tells you about the drug but the *Sun's* doesn't. The *Mirror's* headline has a pun, 'Dopes!', but the *Sun's* doesn't have this.

Comparison of information.

Comparison of headlines.

Comparison of language.

Examiner comment

After a wasted opening sentence, this answer makes three clear comparisons, each covering a different bullet. It's a great shame that it's so brief because, although it just meets the requirements for the D band, there isn't enough range for a higher mark.

Student C

Presentation comparison, supported.

Language comparison, supported.

Both stories have puns in their headlines ('Dopes!' and 'plant') and both have pictures, comparing cannabis with Moss Phlox, but the *Daily Mirror's* is bigger and clearer. The ages of all four people are given in the *Daily Mirror*. but only of the two men in the *Sun*. What the gang said is slightly different – 'Give us the weed' in the *Daily Mirror*. and 'Give us the weed, man' in the *Sun*. There is a lot more information in the *Daily Mirror* (details of being a grandfather and his lacking a sense of smell). The presentation is similar because both stories have large headlines and coloured pictures, but Ivor has put his coat over the same jumper in the *Daily Mirror's* picture.

Extended comment and comparison.

Comparison of information, supported.

Information comparison, supported.

Information comparison, supported.

Presentation comparison, supported by close observation of detail.

Examiner comment

This answer covers all four bullets, makes a range of comparisons and uses detail to support the points being made. It is well into the C band.

MOVING UP THE GRADES

Collate and compare

If you are choosing the texts to compare, make sure you read them all first to select the best ones for the question.

If you are comparing two texts, read the question first, then read the texts to identify specific features and write them down. Then make some direct comparisons, noting similarities and differences.

Student A only makes one specific comment whereas Student B makes several. Student C covers all parts of the question, making comparisons throughout and using closely observed detail to support the points made.

Putting it into practice

Explain what you now know about:
- choosing texts to collate
- comparing texts
- answering the question.

In the future:

- you can practise these skills with any text you come across
- take a few minutes to compare one or more texts
- compare their content
- compare purpose and audience
- compare the language they use and its effect
- compare the presentation they use and its effect.

Section B Writing

Introduction

This section will help you to develop your Writing skills and get the best grade you can in your exam.

In this part of your course you will write for different purposes and audiences. Successful writers make all kinds of choices: not just who they are writing for and the purpose of the text, but what kind of language and presentational devices would be best.

We write all the time. We write lists, notes for other people, text messages and emails to friends. These need to be understood by the person who reads them, so writing clearly and appropriately is important.

This section focuses on specific aspects of writing, one at a time, but we don't often write like this. We need to remember all the different skills all the time, and that is what this book will help you to do.

In the exam you will have to do two pieces of writing, probably for different purposes and maybe for different audiences. In the following chapters you will have a chance to practise the skills you will need.

Write to com... clearly, effe... and imaginatively

Writing for purpose and audience

We write all the time. In the past few weeks you have probably written most of the things listed below:

- lists
- emails
- essays
- notes
- text messages.

Whatever you are writing, it needs to be suited to the task. There's no point taking an essay to go shopping with, or handing in a shopping list for your maths homework. So writing for **purpose** (what it's for) and for **audience** (who it's for) are essential. (You can look back at Chapter 2 in the Reading section to remind yourself about purpose and audience.)

Activity 1

Look at the three everyday tasks below. For each task, decide what the most effective form of communication would be from the list on the right.

Task

1 To complain about a bank charge.
2 To remind yourself what to buy at the supermarket.
3 To arrange a get together with a group of friends.
4 To contact a parent to tell them what time you will be home.

Form

A Hand-written list
B Formal letter
C Email
D A text message

Check your answer

GradeStudio

In your answer to Activity I:

- Did you match each task to one of the forms?
- Did you think about which form would be most effective for each task?

With a shopping list it doesn't matter what order the items come in, because you can cross them off as you buy things. However, some pieces of writing need to be written in the correct order. This is the case in the next activity.

Activity 2

This activity is about Hampton Court – a royal palace near London.

1 Read the statements about Hampton Court below.

2 Now imagine you have to include this information as part of a guidebook. What would be the best order? Number them so they are in the best order. You could follow the hints below if you need to:

- start with general introductory statements
- then put the rest in chronological order
- end with some reasons for visiting Hampton Court.

A Queen Victoria opened Hampton Court to the public in 1838.

B The original Tudor kitchens are well worth a visit.

C Henry VIII re-built and enlarged the palace after 1530.

D Hampton Court is by the River Thames in southwest London.

E Children will enjoy trips round the gardens on the horse-drawn train.

F The maze dates from 1714, but it isn't very scary for modern people.

G Cardinal Wolsey began building the palace in 1514.

H Sir Christopher Wren later extended the palace in the late 1690s.

Write to communicate clearly, effectively and imaginatively

In the last activity you thought about the best way to order pieces of information about Hampton Court. The next activity will ask you to use these pieces of information to write a passage for a guidebook.

Activity 3

Before you start, look at the example of a passage from a guidebook about Stonehenge opposite.

1. Write a short entry for a guidebook on Hampton Court, using the information listed on page 95. Use the bullet points below to help you.
   - Think about the purpose of a guidebook – to inform the reader.
   - Give the passage a heading.
   - Use one or two sub-headings if you like.
   - Arrange the passage into paragraphs to make it easier to read.

2. When you have written your guide to Hampton Court, spend a few minutes checking your spelling, punctuation and grammar.

Check your answer

GradeStudio

In your answer to Activity 3:
- Did you remember the heading?
- Did you use paragraphs?
- Did you check for accuracy?

Stonehenge

How it was built and why

Stonehenge is believed to date from around 3100 BC, although it is likely that it was built in several stages over a period of several hundred years and requiring an estimated 30 million hours of labour!

Why it was built remains the source of much argument and controversy. As a place for druids to hold ritual sacrifices? As an elaborate astronomical calculator? Or simply as a meeting place for people to gather and trade goods? Regardless of why it was built, the moody appeal of Stonehenge has endured to this day, with crowds flocking to the site all year round.

Visiting Stonehenge

Stonehenge is located 9 miles north of Salisbury at the junction of the A303 and A344/360. The nearest train station to Stonehenge is Salisbury. Opening times vary and you are advised to check the website prior to your trip.

Plan your writing

Re-cap

In the last lesson you learned how to make your writing clear and effective. The steps you went through were:

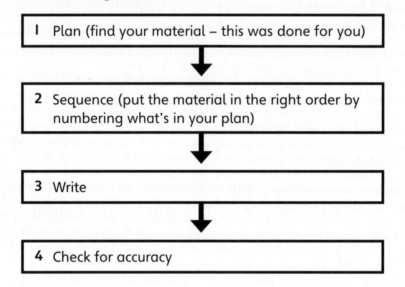

| I | Plan (find your material – this was done for you) |

| 2 | Sequence (put the material in the right order by numbering what's in your plan) |

| 3 | Write |

| 4 | Check for accuracy |

In the exam, many students only do point 3. Doing all of the four things on this list will bring you the best marks you can get.

Activity 1

You are going to write an answer to the following question.

Write an article for a teen magazine explaining what kind of music you like and why.

1 Before you start, write down:
- who the audience for this text is
- what the purpose of this text is.

2 Remember to go through the four stages of clear and effective writing show in the flow chart opposite.

3 Then write your answer.

Stage I Plan

- Note down your ideas for your article.
- Add some detail to your ideas.

Stage 2 Sequence

- Decide on the best order for your ideas and number them.
- Link related ideas by arranging them into paragraphs and give your article a heading.

Stage 3 Write

- Write your article, making sure that you are answering the question all the time.
- Join sentences together to give more variety to interest the reader.

Stage 4 Check for accuracy

- Read your article back to yourself – does it make sense?
- Look out for spelling, punctuation and grammar errors.

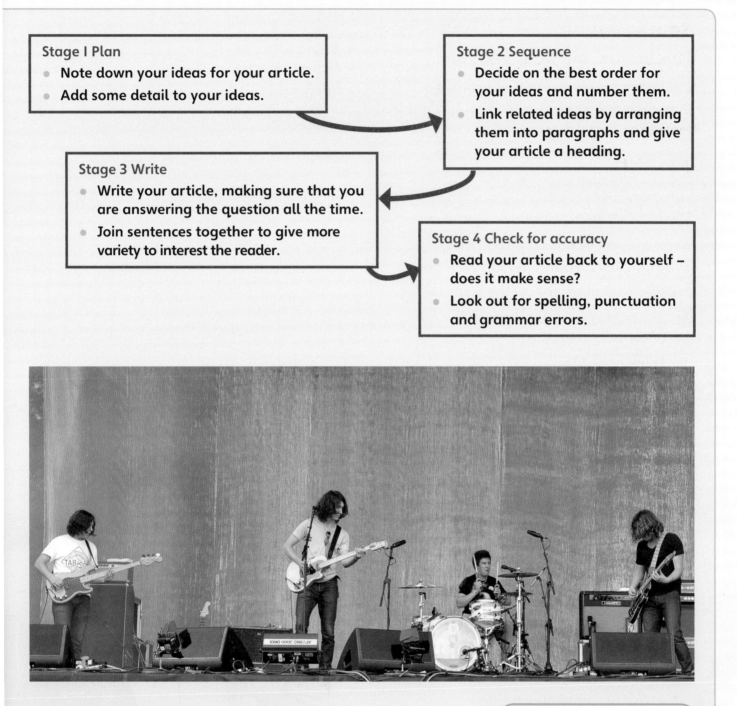

Check your answer

GradeStudio

In your answer to Activity I:
- Did you remember the heading?
- Did you make sure you answered the question all the time?
- Did you put your points in the best order?
- Did you use paragraphs?
- Did you check for accuracy?

Your learning

This lesson will help you to:

- practise an exam-style question
- assess your answer by comparing it with what other students have written.

Activity 1

Write an article for a teenage magazine called 'What makes a young person look good?'

In order to do this, follow the steps below.

1. Write down all your ideas in the form of a spider diagram.

    Think about:
    - cleanliness
    - hair
    - clothes
    - style
    - anything else you can think of.

2. Number all your points so that they come in the best order and form groups that will make paragraphs.

3. When you are writing:
    - start with a heading
    - use paragraphs
    - make it as interesting as you can for your teenage audience
    - use accurate punctuation
    - use accurate spelling.

4. Check your work carefully for accuracy and make any changes you need to.

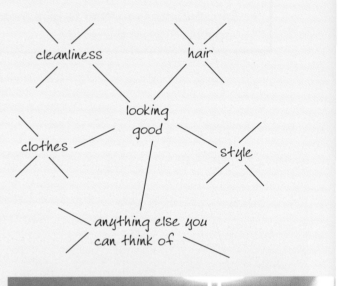

cleanliness   hair

looking
good

clothes   style

anything else you
can think of

Peer/Self-assessment activity

1 Check your answer to the assessment activity. Did you:
- answer the question all the time
- remember the heading
- use paragraphs
- check your work for accuracy?

2 Now grade your answer using the mark scheme below. First, read the sample answers to this task on pages 102–103.

Examiners have to give two separate marks for your writing:

(i) for communication and organisation

(ii) for sentence structure, punctuation and spelling.

(i) communication and organisation

G
- communicates some meaning
- occasional purpose and audience

F
- clear communication of ideas
- more sense of purpose and audience
- some organisational devices
- occasional conscious selection of words

E
- sustained awareness of purpose and audience
- sentences organised into paragraphs
- attempt to use vocabulary for effect

D
- attempts to suit purpose and audience
- begins to engage reader's response
- clear, if mechanical, paragraphing
- conscious use of vocabulary for effect

C
- clear identification with purpose and audience
- begins to sustain reader's response
- evidence of structure
- usually coherent paragraphs
- clear selection of vocabulary for effect

(ii) sentence structure, punctuation and spelling

G
- some sentences
- some simple words spelt correctly

F
- mainly simple and compound sentences
- simple words spelt correctly
- occasional full stops

E
- some accurate sentence demarcation
- some complex words spelt correctly
- accuracy in more than just full stops

D
- range of securely demarcated sentence structures
- accurate spelling of some more complex words
- starts to use range of punctuation

C
- uses sentence forms for effect
- generally secure in spelling
- generally secure in punctuation

Here are two student answers to the activity on page 100. Read the answers together with the examiner comments, and then complete the final peer/self-assessment task.

E grade answer

Student A

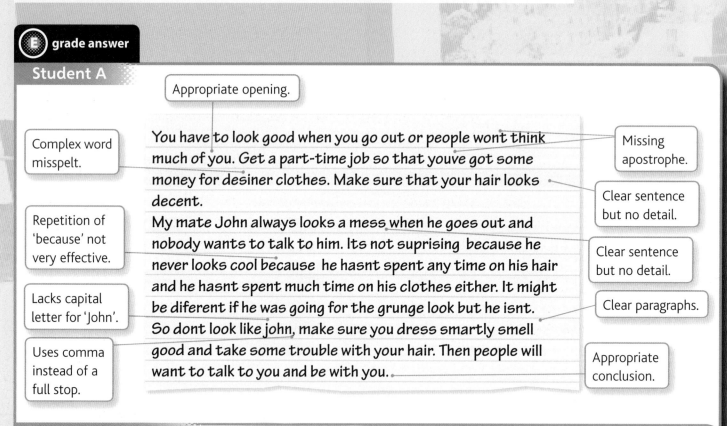

Appropriate opening.

Complex word misspelt.

Missing apostrophe.

Clear sentence but no detail.

Repetition of 'because' not very effective.

Clear sentence but no detail.

Lacks capital letter for 'John'.

Clear paragraphs.

Uses comma instead of a full stop.

Appropriate conclusion.

You have to look good when you go out or people wont think much of you. Get a part-time job so that youve got some money for desiner clothes. Make sure that your hair looks decent.

My mate John always looks a mess when he goes out and nobody wants to talk to him. Its not suprising because he never looks cool because he hasnt spent any time on his hair and he hasnt spent much time on his clothes either. It might be diferent if he was going for the grunge look but he isnt.

So dont look like john, make sure you dress smartly smell good and take some trouble with your hair. Then people will want to talk to you and be with you.

Examiner comment

This suits purpose and audience but it's very general. It needs some precise detail. The anecdote about John is effective but would have been more so with some detail of what he looked like and how he ought to look.

The basic paragraphs are in the right places and divide the writing up effectively with an introduction, the anecdote and a conclusion. There is some vocabulary for effect. It is at the top of the E band for (i) but could have been higher with more specific detail.

This attempts a range of sentence structures, though one has a comma at the end rather than a full stop. Some complex words are used but their spelling is not correct. There are no apostrophes. Only full stops and the hyphen are correct. What a shame that apostrophes were forgotten. It is on the E/F boundary for (ii), though careful checking would surely have pushed it higher than this.

Student B

Direct opening targeting purpose and audience.

You don't have to spend a lot of money to look good. Find out which charity shop the rich people take their clothes to and browse. I've found lots of bargains in one near me and not all the stuff in them is junk. You'd be amazed how many people with lots of money buy something and then get rid of it after they've worn it only once or twice. You can find all the top labels there.

You need to decide what kind of style you want to adopt. It's no use looking at Versace labels if you want the grunge look. Versace doesn't come in grunge. And Laura Ashley is certainly no good for Goths. Look in magazines to find the look you want to adopt and then get out there and look for a cheap version. Even places like Matalan and TK Maxx have some decent things hidden away in corners.

Clothes aren't everything, though. Find a hairstyle which is easy to look after but looks good. Theres no need to spend a fortune in the salon. And make sure you smell good. Everyone likes that.

Sentence form for effect, beginning a sentence with 'and'.

Range of sentence structures.

Third of three sentences beginning with 'you' links paragraphs.

Link between paragraphs.

Detail.

Missing apostrophe.

Short sentences at end for effect.

Examiner comment

Although the first two paragraphs are about clothes, other aspects are briefly considered. The piece is aimed at the right purpose and audience all the way through. The audience is addressed directly and effectively. The paragraphs are clear and coherent and there is some good vocabulary, aimed at a teenage audience, for effect. One punctuation error apart (the missing apostrophe), the spelling and punctuation are accurate. This answer falls at the top of the C band for both (i) and (ii).

Write to communicate clearly, effectively and imaginatively

Higher marks will be given to answers which cover a range of points, sequencing them effectively and using detail as support.

Organisation, sequencing and planning are really important.

Write as accurately as you can and check your work carefully.

Putting it into practice

Explain what you now know about:
- finding ideas
- sequencing them
- using paragraphs
- answering the question
- what makes the difference between Grade E and C answers on writing clearly, effectively and imaginatively.

In the future:

- you can practise planning whatever you write
- you can practise sequencing
- you can practise checking for accuracy.

How to organise information and ideas

Your learning

This lesson will help you to:

- sequence your information and ideas
- plan your writing.

Re-cap

In the last lessons you learned that there are four key stages in creating a successful piece of writing.

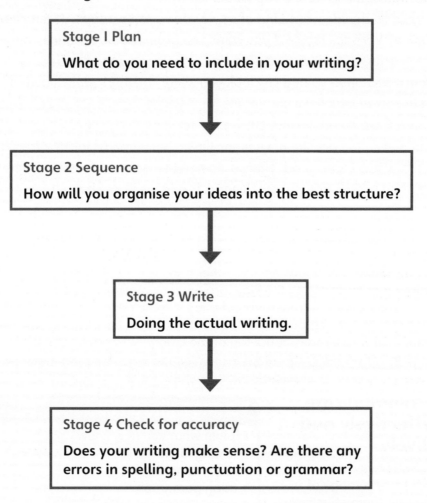

Stage 1 Plan

What do you need to include in your writing?

Stage 2 Sequence

How will you organise your ideas into the best structure?

Stage 3 Write

Doing the actual writing.

Stage 4 Check for accuracy

Does your writing make sense? Are there any errors in spelling, punctuation or grammar?

In the following activities you will learn to plan and sequence your writing.

Activity 1

To help you to present your information and ideas in the best order, you could make a list first and then sequence your points by numbering them.

1 Imagine that you have been asked to write some instructions about how to make a good pot of tea.

Below is the information you need to include.

> **A** Wait a few minutes before you pour the tea.
> **B** Pour the boiling water on the teabags in the teapot.
> **C** Warm the teapot.
> **D** Pour the tea.
> **E** Boil the kettle.
> **F** Put the milk in the cup first.
> **G** Make sure the water is boiling when you put it in the pot.
> **H** Put three teabags in a normal-sized teapot.

2 Number the points so that they are in the right order.

3 Now write some instructions about how to watch a DVD. Make sure you have all the necessary stages, and that they are in the right order.

Check your answer

GradeStudio

In your answer to Activity 1:
- Did you go through all stages?
- Did you put your instructions in the right order?

Paragraphs

Paragraphs are really important. They:

- divide the writing into different sections or stages to make it easier to read
- introduce different parts of the text – for example, a different point in an argument or a different topic
- are linked to help the reader follow what you are writing.

How you use paragraphs depends on what sort of text you are writing.

- Tabloid newspapers use short paragraphs, often just one or two sentences.
- Broadsheet newspapers tend to use longer paragraphs.
- Other articles vary the length of their paragraphs.

See the example below showing use of paragraphs in a tabloid newspaper article.

Opening paragraph to introduce the news story.

New paragraph for the next development in the story – the cat being caught in the act.

New paragraph to introduce quotes from his owner, Louise, about the thieving cat.

It's a purr-fect crime

FELINE GUILTY Henry

CAT STEALS ODD SOCKS

BY ROD CHAYTOR
rchaytor@mirror.co.uk

FOR weeks Henry the cat has been leading a secret life of crime … nicking neighbours' socks then stashing them under his bed.

The serial cat burglar would regularly select them from nearby washing lines, until shocked owner Louise Brandon, 40, caught him bang to rights.

Louise said: 'He jumped over the back fence as bold as brass with a black sock hanging from his mouth. He froze, then walked past me into the house.

'When I followed him, I saw he'd built up a pile of socks behind his bed in the kitchen. There were 51 different socks of all shapes and sizes.'

Mum-of-one Louise has now asked her neighbours in Loughborough, Leics, if they are missing any, but she has so far failed to reunite any missing pairs.

She said: 'It's embarrassing. I've got a bag full of other people's socks.'

And pussyfooting one-year-old Henry shows no sign of kicking his sock habit.

'We took the socks away but he just goes out and steals more,' said Louise.

Baffled expert Sally Walker, of the Woodside Animal Centre in nearby Braunstone Frith, Leicester, said: 'Cats like to bring gifts home – usually birds or mice – but never socks.'

Paragraph used to bring the story up to date.

New paragraph to introduce the opinion of a cat expert.

Activity 2

Imagine you have been asked to write an article for a magazine about living a healthy lifestyle.

1 First, decide who your audience is. Who is going to read it?

2 Write down your ideas about how to live a healthy lifestyle in a list or spider diagram.

Below are some possible ideas.

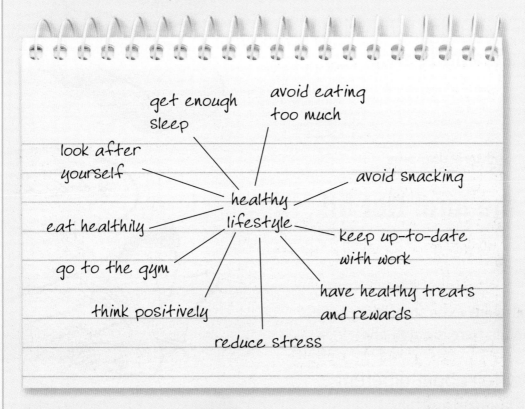

get enough sleep

avoid eating too much

look after yourself

avoid snacking

healthy lifestyle

eat healthily

keep up-to-date with work

go to the gym

have healthy treats and rewards

think positively

reduce stress

3 Write a sentence for each idea.

4 Decide:

- which ideas are linked
- which ideas show different aspects of the topic.

5 Combine the sentences with ideas that are linked to form paragraphs. You may be able to join sentences with linked ideas using a conjunction. For example, 'It is important to look after yourself and get enough sleep'.

6 Group together paragraphs that cover the same aspects of the topic.

Beginnings and endings

How you begin and end a text is really important. For example, good headlines for newspaper articles draw the reader in and make them want to read the rest of the article.

The **first sentence** is also important: it has to make the reader want to read on. For example, here is a very dull opening:

> In this article I am going to be writing about living a healthy lifestyle

And here is a more interesting one:

> **Off with the lard! Get fit!**

The **ending**, too, needs to be something for the reader to remember. Here is a dull one:

> So I have written about different ways about living healthily.

And here is a more interesting one:

> **Blueberries and the gym for me!**

Activity 3

1   Look back at the planning you did in Activity 2 on page 107 for the magazine article on healthy living.

2   Decide on a headline for your article that will draw the reader in.

3   Now think of three opening sentences you could use. Choose the best one. Remember: it has to make the reader want to read on.

4   Now think of three possible last sentences that will bring your article to a good conclusion. Remember: it has to be something that will stick in the reader's mind.

5   Now you're ready to write your article. Remember to:
   - write your headline
   - start with a catchy opening
   - use paragraphs
   - find some links between paragraphs
   - end with an interesting sentence.

Check your answer

GradeStudio

In your answer to Activity 3:
- Did you plan carefully enough?
- Did you put your ideas in the best order?
- Did you check your spelling?
- Did you check your punctuation?
- Did you correct any errors?

Assessment practice

Your learning
This lesson will help you to:
- practise an exam-style question
- assess your answer by looking at other responses.

Activity 1

In Activity 3 on page 109 you wrote an article using continuous prose and paragraphs. In the exam, you might be asked to write an advice sheet or an information sheet or an instruction sheet. These often use:

- a title
- headings
- sub-headings
- bullets
- boxes (maybe).

Write an information sheet for people your own age about healthy living. You can use the same information you used for Activity 3, but this time your purpose and audience are different. Follow the tips below to help you.

1 Think of a suitable heading.

2 Decide what sub-headings you could use. You might start by using these:
- Food
- Exercise
- Sleep.

3 Now write your information sheet, thinking carefully about:
- language suitable for your audience
- sentence length and structures
- presenting your information clearly
- using accurate punctuation
- using a range of different punctuation marks.

4 Check your work carefully for accuracy and make any changes you need to.

Peer/Self-assessment activity

1 Check your answer to the assessment activity. Did you:
- sequence your ideas before you began
- give it a suitable heading
- start with a catchy opening
- use sub-headings
- use a catchy sentence at the end
- check your punctuation and spelling for accuracy?

2 Now grade your answer using the mark scheme below. First read the sample answers to this task on pages 112–113.

Examiners have to give two separate marks for your writing, but here you are just concentrating on the communication and organisation.

G
▶ communicates some meaning
▶ occasional sense of purpose and audience

F
▶ clear communication of ideas
▶ more sense of purpose and audience
▶ some organisational devices
▶ occasional conscious selection of words

E
▶ sustained awareness of purpose and audience
▶ sentences organised into paragraphs or sections
▶ attempt to use vocabulary for effect

D
▶ attempts to suit purpose and audience
▶ begins to engage reader's response
▶ clear, if mechanical, sections or paragraphs
▶ conscious use of vocabulary for effect

C
▶ clear identification with purpose and audience
▶ begins to sustain reader's response
▶ evidence of structure
▶ usually coherent paragraphs/sections
▶ clear selection of vocabulary for effect

Here are two student answers to the activity on pages 110–111. Read the answers together with the examiner comments, and then complete the final peer/self-assessment task.

Student A

Direct address.

Appropriate heading.

Clear teenage audience.

Appropriate sub-headings.

Banish the blues

The way to feel good about yourself is to live healthily. And it can be fun.

Timetable

Make sure you get enough sleep at night so that you're fresh in the mornings and ready to work and live life to the full. Staying up late just makes you feel bad. Get yourself organised. Do your homework as soon as you get home, spend less time in front of the telly or playing on the internet and you will enjoy life so much more.

Food and drink

All those crisps, chips and fizzy drinks are bad for you, so avoid them. If you eat lots of stuff full of fat and sugar you will end up fat yourself but not so sweet. Make sure you eat your five a day fruit and veggies and drink water. Even the diet coke you so love is full of carcinogens to replace the sugar. They are just as bad for you as the cans with five teaspoons of sugar in them. Make sure you eat regular meals, too. Have a decent breakfast and then a tuna sandwich for lunch instead of all that rubbish you're used to eating. Then you can enjoy dinner when you get home. Remember: snacks between meals are forbidden!

Exercise

30 minutes of aerobic exercise a day is called for, so play football, run, do a dance class, walk or run home and you will soon feel better. Don't think of this as being healthy. Just think of it as having fun.

Live

Get rid of the pizza and chips. Have blueberries and tofu instead. Get off your ass and into your running shoes. Have a decent night's sleep and I promise you will feel on top of the world.

Catchy conclusion, directly aimed at audience.

Specific detailed information.

Examiner comment

This is detailed, well organised, clearly structured and maintains purpose and audience throughout. It meets all the C grade criteria.

Student B

This information sheet is about healthy living. You need to live healthily in order to keep fit and well. The kind of food you eat affects how you feel. You should also get regular exercise. Don't eat too much or you will get fat. Try walking to school instead of getting the bus. Eat the healthy option for lunch.

> Dull start.

> This should have gone with the other sentences about food.

Examiner comment

This certainly communicates meaning, but there is little sense of audience (except the mention of school). The material is about healthy living, but it is all very general. The sentences are all similar lengths and rather monotonous. There are no organisational features (except 'also'). The words are appropriate but not very individual or interesting. The answer is in the F band.

How to organise information and ideas

The secret – and it's not much of a secret – to this is to have a well-oiled system.

Gather your ideas first, then sequence them, and then while you are writing you can think about expressing yourself as well as possible.

When you get into the exam room, plan, plan, plan!

Putting it into practice

Explain what you now know about:
- organising information
- organising ideas
- checking your work for accuracy
- what makes the difference between Grade F and C answers in terms of organising information and ideas.

In the future:

- you can practise planning and sequencing whatever you write
- you can practise choosing devices to present your material clearly and attractively
- you can practise checking your own work for accuracy.

Structure

The **structure** of a text means how the writing is divided up and presented on the page. Some texts, like information texts and advertisements, often break up the text into different sections. They might use:

- pictures
- boxes
- bullet points
- colour.

Other texts, such as magazine articles, might have a block of writing that has:

- a beginning
- a middle with several stages
- an end.

Activity 1

1. Read the advertisement opposite. It is from a brochure by the National Trust to promote its attractions in Cornwall.

2. The advertisement is divided into six different numbered sections. Match the sections with the descriptions below.

A Picture with caption	**D** Heading
B Opening times	**E** Map
C List of attractions	**F** Entrance charges and location

3. Each section uses a different method of presentation. Match the sections with one of the descriptions below.

G Bright colours; white writing on purple background
H Black diagram on pale blue background
I Black print beginning with bold
J Bullet points
K Box with blue columns
L White writing on wide purple background

Lanhydrock ♿⬚🚻🚼 (in woods and park)

Map ref: 9

(1)

- Magnificent late Victorian country house, atmospheric home of the Agar-Robartes family
- Fifty rooms to explore, revealing fascinating aspects of life & the inner workings of this wealthy well-run household
- Highlights incl. great kitchen, evocative nursery wing & 17th century Long Gallery with plaster ceiling depicting biblical scenes

(2)

- Large formal & woodland garden incl. Victorian parterre, stunning magnolias, camellias & rhododendrons
- Superb parkland setting in the Fowey valley, with miles of walks through woods & along the river

(3)

Gift Aid Admission: Adult £9.90, child £4.95, family £24.75, family (1 adult) £14.85. Groups adult £8.40. Garden & grounds only: adult £5.60, child £2.80.
Nr Bodmin PL30 5AD
E lanhydrock@nationaltrust.org.uk
T 01208 265950 (estate 265211)
🚃 Bodmin Parkway 1¾ miles, lovely walk

The great house of Cornwall: 'Upstairs Downstairs' brought to life

(5)

(4)

Opening arrangements 2008			NB: Bold – open
House	15 Mar–2 Nov	11–5.30 (5 from 1 Oct)	M **T W T F S S**
Garden	All year	10–6	**M T W T F S S**
Shop & refreshments	5 Jan–3 Feb	11–4	M T W T F **S S**
	9 Feb–14 Mar	11–4	**M T W T F S S**
	15 Mar–2 Nov	11–5.30 (5 from 1 Oct)	**M T W T F S S**
	3 Nov–24 Dec	11–4	**M T W T F S S**
	27 Dec–31 Dec	11–4	**M T** W T F **S S**

Also open BH Mons & Mons in August. Plant sales open daily 1 Mar – 2 Nov. **Refreshments available from 10.30 in main season.** Shop & refreshments are inside tariff area. Tel. for specific details of restaurant opening,

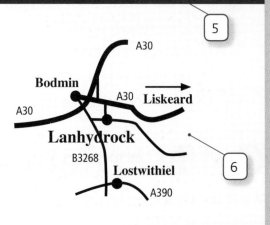

(6)

Activity 2

Choose a place that people can visit and write a one-page advertisement for it.

1. Write a list of the sorts of information you are going to include.
2. Sequence the list.
3. Divide the information into different sections.
4. Divide your page into the number of sections you need.
5. Decide how you are going to present each section. You could use some of the following:

- illustrations
- boxes
- different sizes and shapes of section
- bullet points
- paragraphs
- bold and italic print.

Structuring your writing

Re-cap

In the last lesson you looked at how an advertisement was structured. You used this to help you structure your own piece of writing. In this lesson you will do something similar, but this time you will write your own newspaper article.

Activity 1

A newspaper article is also divided up into sections, but these are in the form of paragraphs.

1 Read the article from *Sky Sports Magazine*.

2 Find the following structural features in the article:

- general introduction to subject
- large headline
- sub-heading for article
- information about Qualifying School.
- update on Michelle Wie

Golf's cruellest game

When it comes to pressure nothing beats the emotions at Q-School

At age 12 Michelle Wie became the youngest player in a pro event. At 14, Arnold Palmer said: 'She's going to influence golf as much as Tiger.' At 16, she was worth millions of dollars.

Now 19, things are a little different for Wie. She failed to reach the Top 80 money winners on the LPGA Tour and so this month she's playing in 'Golf's Cruellest Tournament', aka Q-School. If she gets through each round and finishes in the Top 30 she's back on the Tour. If not, she's out in the wilderness for the next year.

Each major tour has a Qualifying School and it's merciless – one stroke the difference between making your fortune and not. At this year's European Tour Q-School, more than 700 players paid £1,250 for their chance to reach the Final stage in Spain in November.

Things aren't as rosy for Michelle Wie these days

There, around 300 golfers competed over six rounds for 25 Tour places.

In 1994, Sky Sports' Robert Lee went to Q-School after missing a birdie at the Volvo Masters. He said: 'Everyone knows if you have a bad year you have to come back, but it doesn't make it easier.' At least Lee got his Tour card back at the first attempt. Plenty of other golfers will end 2008 having failed to make it, and will turn their back on the game for good.

ON SKY SPORTS: GOLF NIGHT THURSDAY 11 DECEMBER, 7PM

The article is structured quite simply. It has:

- a headline
- a sub-heading to the article
- an introduction to Michelle Wie
- an update on what has happened to her
- information about Qualifying School
- a conclusion.

This is a useful structure to use in your own writing:

- a headline
- an introduction
- two (or three or four) middle paragraphs
- a conclusion.

Activity 2

Now write your own article using this structure. Choose a person you admire and write a short informative article about them.

Check your answer

GradeStudio

In your answer to Activity 2:
- Did you plan before you started to write?
- Did you put your ideas in the best order?
- Did you use your paragraphs effectively?

Language

The language you use needs to suit your text, audience and purpose – in other words, **what** you are writing, **who** you are writing for and **why** you are writing it.

For example, if you are writing to instruct you would use words that tell people what they should do, such as:

- 'you should...'
- 'you must...'
- 'make sure you...'.

If you are writing to persuade, you might use rhetorical questions (questions that don't need an answer), such as:

- 'Have you ever thought of...?'
- 'Why don't you...?'
- 'Wouldn't it be better if you...?'

Most writers use a range of techniques to get their readers interested.

Activity 1

1. Read the letter opposite. It is a letter written to a newspaper by a fireman, explaining why he thinks the work he does is worth the £30,000 a year he is paid. Identify an example of each of the following:
   - rhetorical question
   - repetition of 'I have'
   - groups of three
   - repeated words within sentences
   - words repeated in related sentences
   - slang
   - emotional appeals to the reader.

2. Think about why each of these features has been used. What effect does each of them have?

The Guardian

Am I worth £30,000?

Am I worth £30,000? In my career I have been taught skills to save life, prolong life and to know when to walk away when there is no life left. I have taken courses to fight fire from within, above and below. I can cut a car apart in minutes and I can educate your sons and daughters to save their own lives.

No matter what the emergency, I am part of a team that always comes when you call. I run in when all my instincts tell me to run away. I have faced death in cars with petrol pouring over me while the engine was ticking with the heat. I have lain on my back inside a house fire and watched the flames roar across the ceiling above me. I have climbed and I have crawled to save life and I have stood and wept while we buried a fellow firefighter.

I have been the target for yobs throwing stones and punches at me while I do my job. I have been the first person to intercept a parent who knows their son is in the car we are cutting up, and I know he is dead. I have served my time, damaged my body and seen things that I hope you never will. I have never said 'No, I'm more important than you', and walked away.

Am I worth £30k? Maybe now your answer is no. But when that drunk smashes into your car, or the candle burns down too low, or your child needs help, you will find I'm worth every last penny.

Jay Curson
Firefighter, Nottingham

Activity 2

Imagine that you are doing a job which you think is useful and important.

Write a letter to a magazine, persuading your reader that what you do is important and that it is worth the money you are paid.

You can use some of the language techniques that you identified in Activity 1. Before you start to write, make sure that you:

- gather your ideas
- put your ideas in a logical order
- decide on your paragraphs
- use interesting language.

Check your answer

GradeStudio

In your answer to Activity 2:
- Did you structure your letter carefully?
- Did you have an interesting opening?
- Did you use paragraphs?
- Did you use a number of the language features you identified in Activity 1?
- Did you have an interesting conclusion?

Your learning

This lesson will help you to:

- practise an exam-style question
- assess your answer by looking at other responses.

Activity 1

Write a letter to the Chair of the Governors of your school or college, arguing for or against school uniform.

Before you begin:

- Decide whether your letter will be for or against school uniform.
- Gather all your ideas together. You might want to use a spider diagram to help with this.
- Decide which are your best ideas – which ones make the best case for your argument?
- Sequence your ideas – for example by numbering them on your spider diagram.
- Decide on your paragraphs.
- Use language suitable for the Chair of Governors to read.
- Think about the features of a formal letter.
- Make sure you are always making an argument and interesting your listener.

Peer/Self-assessment activity

MAKE THE GRADE

1 Check your answer to the assessment activity. Did you:
  • sequence your ideas before you began
  • write a suitable opening and sign-off to the letter
  • use paragraphs
  • write in formal standard English
  • use appropriate language?

2 Now grade your answer using the mark scheme below. First, read the sample answers to this task on pages 122–123.

Examiners have to give two separate marks for your writing, but here you are just concentrating on the communication and organisation.

G
▶ communicates some meaning
▶ occasional purpose and audience

F
▶ clear communication of ideas
▶ more sense of purpose and audience
▶ some organisational devices
▶ occasional conscious selection of words

E
▶ sustained awareness of purpose and audience
▶ sentences organised into paragraphs or sections
▶ attempt to use vocabulary for effect

D
▶ attempts to suit purpose and audience
▶ begins to engage reader's response
▶ clear, if mechanical, sections or paragraphs
▶ conscious use of vocabulary for effect

C
▶ clear identification with purpose and audience
▶ begins to sustain reader's response
▶ evidence of structure
▶ usually coherent paragraphs/sections
▶ clear selection of vocabulary for effect

Here are two student answers to the activity on pages 120–121. Read the answers together with the examiner comments, and then complete the final peer/self-assessment task.

Student A

Anytown High School
Some Road
Anytown
ZB2 3XS
3 March 2010

Dear Chair of Governors,

Because you have asked students what they think, I am writing to express my support for your present policy of maintaining high standards of school uniform.

School uniform prepares us for the world of work where we will have to wear clothes appropriate to our job. Many of us will go on to jobs which require uniform in order to make us look smart and to fit in with a corporate identity, so it is no bad thing to get us used to this while we are at school.

Although school uniform is expensive and has constantly to be renewed and replaced because we are growing, nevertheless your system of having grants for students whose parents cannot afford to buy uniforms allows everyone to look the same and therefore be treated the same. It is an effective way of ensuring equal opportunities.

School uniform encourages responsibility, too. We can be identified on the way to and from school and we have the reputation of the school to uphold.

Please keep school uniform. It is good for us.

Yours faithfully,

A Student

Annotations:
- All the necessary letter features, appropriately used.
- Clear opening.
- Effective paragraphs with developed points.
- Effective formal vocabulary throughout.
- Clear, punchy conclusion.
- Appropriate sign-off

Examiner comment

This is detailed, well organised, clearly structured and maintains purpose and audience throughout. Its structure and language are both clear and effective. It meets all the C criteria.

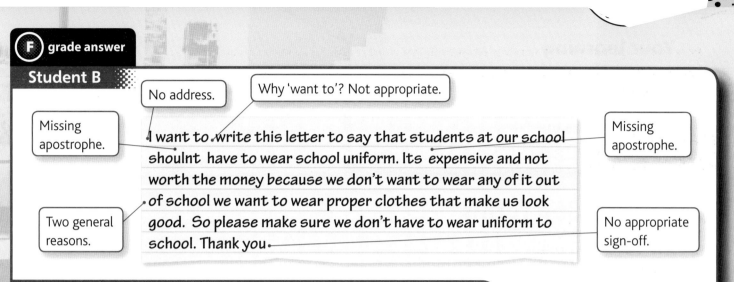

Student B

No address.

Why 'want to'? Not appropriate.

Missing apostrophe.

Missing apostrophe.

Two general reasons.

No appropriate sign-off.

I want to write this letter to say that students at our school shoulnt have to wear school uniform. Its expensive and not worth the money because we don't want to wear any of it out of school we want to wear proper clothes that make us look good. So please make sure we don't have to wear uniform to school. Thank you

Examiner comment

This isn't really a letter because it doesn't have the necessary salutation and sign-off. A few points are made but they are not developed. There are no paragraphs. The language is simple and not particularly appropriate for the Chair of Governors. The communication is clear. The answer is in the F band.

Use language and structure

If you plan and sequence your material before you start to write, you can structure it effectively. If you don't, you can't.

So write your ideas down first, then sequence them. In this way you will have decided on your structure before you begin to write.

When you start to write you can then think about using the most effective language for your purpose.

Putting it into practice

Explain what you now know about:
- structuring your work
- using presentational devices to help you structure
- using paragraphs to help you structure
- using effective and interesting language
- checking your work for accuracy
- what makes the difference between Grade F and C answers in terms of using structure and language.

In the future:

- you can practise planning and structuring whatever you write
- you can practise choosing devices to present your material clearly and attractively
- you can practise using effective and interesting language in whatever you write.

Introducing forms

When we talk about the **form** of a text we mean what kind of text it is. You have already looked at a wide range of forms, especially in the Reading section of this book. You can use these to help you in your own writing.

Some of the main forms you may be asked to write in the exam are:

- letters
- articles
- information sheets
- advice sheets
- emails.

Letters

Below is an example of the beginning of a formal letter. Its features are labelled in the boxes.

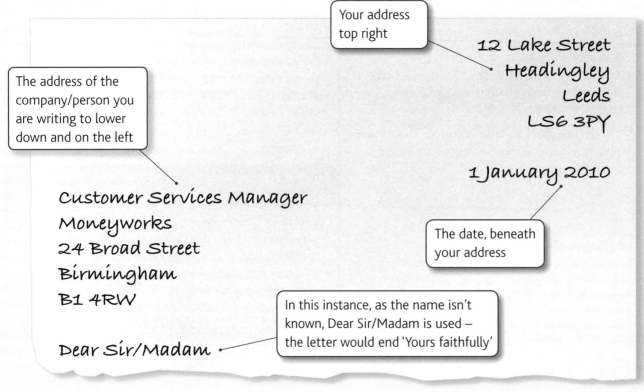

Your address top right

12 Lake Street
Headingley
Leeds
LS6 3PY

1 January 2010

The date, beneath your address

The address of the company/person you are writing to lower down and on the left

Customer Services Manager
Moneyworks
24 Broad Street
Birmingham
B1 4RW

Dear Sir/Madam

In this instance, as the name isn't known, Dear Sir/Madam is used – the letter would end 'Yours faithfully'

If you are writing to a company and don't know the name of the person you are writing to, you need to:

- put your address
- put the date
- put the address the letter is going to
- start with 'Dear Sir' or 'Dear Sir/Madam'
- sign off with 'Yours faithfully'
- sign your name
- then print your name if your signature isn't easy to read.

If you are writing to someone whose name you know, you do the same, except:

- you put 'Dear Mr/Mrs...' instead of 'Dear Sir' or 'Dear Sir/Madam'
- you end 'Yours sincerely' instead of 'Yours faithfully'.

If you are writing to a friend:

- you don't include their address
- you might start 'Dear Chris'
- you might be more informal and end with 'Love' or 'Cheers'.

Activity 1

Now write just the beginning and ending of each of the following.

1 A letter to a friend.
2 A business letter to someone whose name you don't know.
3 A business letter to someone whose name you do know.

Check your answer

GradeStudio

In your answers to Activity 1:

- Did you set out your letters as in the examples above?
- Did you use 'Dear Sir/Madam', 'Dear ...' correctly?
- Did you use the correct sign-off?
- Did you include the date?

Information and advice sheets

Your learning

This lesson will help you to:

- understand the features of information and advice sheets
- write your own information and advice sheet.

HOW TO...

The purpose of an information and advice sheet is to get information to the reader clearly and directly. They often include features such as:

- headings and subheadings
- different styles (bold, italic, capitals, underlining, font size, colour)
- bullet points and other listing devices
- language that informs, explains and instructs
- pictures and diagrams to help explain and inform.

Here is an example of an information and advice sheet. Look at its features, labelled in the boxes.

Serve like Rafael Nadal

Analyse the top stars' sporting skills yourself using Sky⁺

Nadal is best known for his punishing groundstrokes, but as Sky Sports analyst Mark Petchey explains, his serve is now a weapon too.

'I wouldn't say it's his most natural shot, but it's the shot over the last 12 months that's enabled him to win Majors outside the French. When he first came on to the tour it all looked very jerky. It didn't look a fluid shot.

'Now his timing has improved immeasurably. He's got a lot more power on it now, a lot more snap, a lot more speed with the racquet head.'

Here, Mark tells us how to serve like the soaring Spaniard...

Keep your balance 'The key component of a serve is balance. In terms of transferring your weight – back to load up the power, then down with your legs so you can explode up off the surface to get maximum height to hit your serve. And that whole motion needs to be well balanced to that you can make a high number of serves.'

Apply pressure 'He's started serving into the body a lot more this year I've noticed. It's not going to get him a lot of free points but it's going to set up the point for his forehand.'

Sustain the pressure 'The thing he does that other players have problems with is his second serve. It's very difficult to attack.

He puts a lot of spin on it. It looks a bit slow on TV but Andy [Murray] says it's very difficult to actually take a clean hit at it. It's moving around all over the place.'

Adapt to the surface... 'He goes for his serve more on grass. He tries to hit his first serve a lot harder. On clay – he's not looking for cheap points. He's looking to get his opponent off the court and then he can start moving them around with his groundies.'

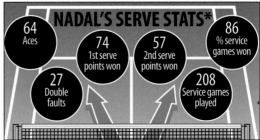

NADAL'S SERVE STATS*

64 Aces

74 1st serve points won

57 2nd serve points won

86 % service games won

27 Double faults

208 Service games played

...and the opponent 'If you watch him play Andy, he'll serve more body and forehand than out wide for the backhand. Against Roger [Federer], he'll go for a very high percentage into Roger's backhand.'

Swap hands 'Being a left-hander is a big advantage – it's a completely different kind of spin that comes at the right-hander – it curls into our forehand on the deuce side. On the ad side he'll serve and volley on big points swinging you off the court. He really does use his serve effectively.'

LIVE ON SKY SPORTS: ATP WORLD TOUR MASTERS 1000: MONTE CARLO, STARTS MON 13 APR 9.30PM SS3; ROME, STARTS MON 27 APR NOON SS2

Pictures showing you stages in the serve.

Boxed information about the serve.

Activity 1

Write your own information sheet about something you know a lot about, telling people how to do it. You could choose a sport or a hobby, or any other interest.

Remember to:

- list your ideas first
- sequence them
- decide on your heading
- decide on your sub-headings
- use bullet points or other listing devices
- think about the type of language you need to use to inform and persuade your reader
- think about any illustrations you want
- make a box and write in what illustrations you want.

Check your answer

GradeStudio

In your answer to Activity I:

- Did you plan and sequence your material first?
- Did you use a heading and sub-headings?
- Did you think carefully about the language you used?
- Did you think carefully about the illustrations you used?

Articles

Articles can appear in newspapers, magazines, on websites and many other places. If you are asked to write an article, you need to think about the following things:

- where it might be printed
- its purpose – e.g. to inform, persuade, entertain and so on
- its intended audience.

Then you need to make choices about:

- the language you'll use
- headings, sub-headings and any other presentational features
- how you will structure the article into paragraphs.

Activity 1

1. Look at the example of an article opposite. Some of the main features of the article are highlighted for you.

2. Now write your own article for a tabloid newspaper, with the title 'What interests teenagers'.

   Make sure that you:
   - gather your ideas first
   - sequence your ideas
   - decide what is going to be in each paragraph
   - decide how you might use images and captions
   - have a snappy introduction
   - have several paragraphs in the middle – one per idea, maybe
   - have an interesting conclusion for the last paragraph.

   GradeStudio

   ### Check your answer

   In your answer to Activity 1:
   - Did you plan and sequence first?
   - Did you use a headline?
   - Did you arrange your paragraphs in the best order?
   - Did you have an interesting start and finish?

Name of writer.

Headline to grab your attention and tell you what the article is about.

Snappy introduction.

Short paragraphs because it's in a free newspaper (a tabloid).

The writing is in paragraphs, making it easier to read

METRO

Birthday boy Bob keeps on building

By **Miles Erwin**

Can he party? Yes, he can!

Bob The Builder, an inspiration for hundreds of thousands of junior DIY-ers, is turning ten.

The world's most famous craftsman celebrates a decade on the nation's TV screens this Thursday.

During his 16 series and 260 episodes, Bob has rebuilt Bobsville umpteen times over with the help of sidekick Wendy, Farmer Pickles and his construction crew of Scoop, Muck, Lofty and the rest.

He was the brainchild of Keith Chapman who dreamed up the catchphrase 'Can we fix it? Yes, we can!' Chapman said: 'I saw a JCB digging up the road in Wimbledon and stood there and sketched it on my way to work. I sketched other machines, a dump truck, a crane, a cement mixer and a steam roller.

'I felt they needed a father figure and came up with Bob. But it was a toss-up between Bill the Builder or Bob the Builder. And Bob won.'

Such is his worldwide appeal, there's reputedly not a nation on the planet that hasn't succumbed. His shows have been translated into 45 languages.

In Brazil, he's Bob o Construtor, in France he's Bob le Bricoleur, in Norway Byggmester Bob and Mojster Miha in Slovenia.

Among the stars who have graced his show are Sir Elton John, Chris Evans and Ulrika Jonsson.

And he's not just a TV star, as his 2000 song Can We Fix It? went to No.1.

'I knew when I first drew Bob the Builder, I had created a very special character but I never dreamed he would be this much of a success,' added Chapman.

Incidentally, if Bob was real, he would be just outside the top 100 richest people in the world, with earnings of £2.5 billion.

Amusing conclusion.

Pictures to make it look more interesting for the readers

Your learning

This lesson will help you to:

- understand the features of text messages and emails
- write your own text messages and emails, using the right level of formality.

Text messages

Text messages are often very short and use abbreviations, but their meaning should still be clear. They are usually a very informal way of communicating. Sometimes, however, text messages need to be a bit more formal – for example, when you don't know the person very well.

Below are an informal and a less informal text. Read them and look at their features labelled in the boxes.

Informal text

Less informal text

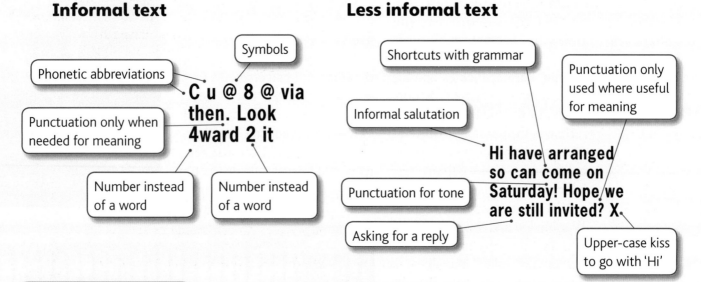

Symbols

Phonetic abbreviations

Punctuation only when needed for meaning

C u @ 8 @ via then. Look 4ward 2 it

Number instead of a word

Number instead of a word

Shortcuts with grammar

Punctuation only used where useful for meaning

Informal salutation

Hi have arranged so can come on Saturday! Hope we are still invited? X

Punctuation for tone

Asking for a reply

Upper-case kiss to go with 'Hi'

Activity 1

Now write an informal text message and a more formal one, both replying to an invitation to meet somewhere.

Check your answer

GradeStudio

In your answer to Activity I:
- Did you use abbreviations?
- Did you use punctuation in order to avoid misunderstanding?
- Did you make sure your meaning was always clear?

Emails

Like text messages, **emails** can be an informal way of communicating with friends.

Many emails are also used for business and use standard English, because you don't want the person receiving it to think you can't write properly!

Formal emails:

- are often short and to the point
- don't have addresses because the email addresses are on the email
- don't have a date because the computer tells you the date and time of sending
- have a salutation
- have a sign-off.

Here is an example of a formal email. Read it and look at its features labelled in the boxes. You will see that it's just like an informal letter without the addresses and date.

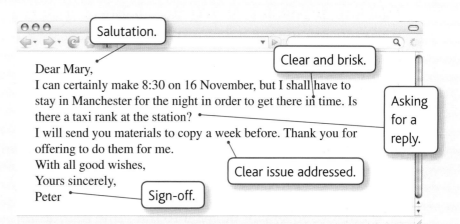

Salutation.

Clear and brisk.

Dear Mary,
I can certainly make 8:30 on 16 November, but I shall have to stay in Manchester for the night in order to get there in time. Is there a taxi rank at the station?
I will send you materials to copy a week before. Thank you for offering to do them for me.
With all good wishes,
Yours sincerely,
Peter

Asking for a reply.

Clear issue addressed.

Sign-off.

Activity 2

Write an email in reply to this one from Mrs Jane Johnson, Deputy Head of your school.

Dear Student,
I want to invite some responsible students to be part of a committee to organise an end-of-year event for Year 11 students. I am hoping that those who come forward will put in some time in meetings and be prepared to take a leading role in the organisation of the event.
Please let me know if you are interested in being part of the committee and what you could contribute to the group.
Yours faithfully,
Jane Johnson

Check your answer

GradeStudio

In your answer to Activity 2:

- Did you plan before you started to write?
- Did you put your ideas in the best order?
- Did you reply to both issues?
- Did you use the correct features of a formal email?

Your learning

This lesson will help you to:

- practise an exam-style question
- assess your answer by looking at other responses.

Activity 1

Your local newspaper has recently published an article saying that young people nowadays spend their time vandalising the neighbourhood and terrorising older people.

Write a letter to the editor of the local newspaper, expressing your own point of view about this.

Here are some tips to help you write your letter.

- First think about the points you want to make in your letter. Make a list.
- Next, decide on the order of your points and number them. Group similar points into the same paragraph.
- Now you can start to write your letter. Remember to use the correct features of a letter:
    - your name and address and the date
    - the address the letter is going to
    - the correct opening – for example, 'Dear Sir/Madam/ Mr/Mrs'
    - the correct sign off
    - sign and print your name.

    Look back at the advice on pages 114–115 if you are not sure.

- Finally, check your writing. Does it all make sense? Are there any spelling, punctuation or grammar errors?

Peer/Self-assessment activity

1 Check your answer to the assessment activity. Did you:
- sequence your ideas before you began
- write a suitable opening and sign-off to the letter
- use paragraphs
- write in formal standard English
- use appropriate language?

2 Now grade your answer, using the mark scheme below. First, read the sample answers to this task on pages 134–135. For this question you are just concentrating on the communication and organisation of your writing.

G
- ▶ communicates some meaning
- ▶ occasional purpose and audience
- ▶ occasional sense of a letter

F
- ▶ clear communication of ideas
- ▶ more sense of purpose and audience
- ▶ some letter features
- ▶ occasional conscious selection of words

E
- ▶ sustained awareness of purpose and audience
- ▶ sentences organised into paragraphs or sections
- ▶ attempt to use vocabulary for effect
- ▶ some features of a letter to the editor

D
- ▶ attempts to suit purpose and audience
- ▶ begins to engage reader's response
- ▶ clear, if mechanical, use of letter features
- ▶ conscious use of vocabulary for effect

C
- ▶ clear identification with purpose and audience
- ▶ begins to sustain reader's response
- ▶ evidence of structure
- ▶ accurate use of letter features
- ▶ usually coherent paragraphs/sections
- ▶ clear selection of vocabulary for effect

Here are two student answers to the activity on pages 132–133. Read the answers together with the examiner comments, and then complete the final peer/self-assessment task.

Student A

Clear opening directing editor's attention to the article.

All letter features present and correct.

Short, appropriate paragraphs, each dealing with a different aspect of the topic.

Pithy conclusion.

61 Some Road
Anytown
ZB2 3XS
3 March 2010

Dear Editor,

You published an article last week about young people vandalising their neighbourhoods and terrorising young people. A tiny minority of young people might be like this, but most of us are not.

We hang around together because we have friends. We hang around bus stops because we have to use public transport and we all come out of school at the same time.

Most young people care about their futures and work hard at school and with their homework. Many young people look after and care for older people.

The writer should not dismiss all young people on the basis of a bad experience with one or two.

Yours faithfully,
A Student

Appropriate sign-off.

Examiner comment

This response achieves all the C descriptors. The letter form is confidently and accurately used. Although the comments are not fully extended or developed, the points are all sensible and clearly address the points made in the original article.

Student B

No salutation.

Thats a load of rubbish young people dont go around vandalising and creating trubble they are just trying to live their lives like anybody else you shouldn't print stuff like this about young people which isnt true you should find out the facts first before you write stuff.

No sign-off.

Expresses point of view.

Examiner comment

While this student has something to say and expresses an opinion, there is very little sense of a letter. There are none of the required letter features and no punctuation at all. Something relevant is written, but nothing is explained or developed and there is no evidence for any of the opinions. In terms of using letter form, this answer is very weak. Because it writes something relevant to the topic and because it implies that it is writing to the editor of the newspaper, it just moves into the G band.

MOVING UP THE GRADES

Use and adapt forms

The key to success with the use and adaptation of forms is to be familiar with their characteristics and to use their features.

Student A uses all the necessary features confidently and accurately but Student B doesn't do this at all.

Putting it into practice

Explain what you now know about:
- using and adapting different forms
- planning your work
- using paragraphs to help you structure
- what makes the difference between Grade G and C answers in terms of using and adapting forms.

In the future:

- you can practise planning and structuring whatever you write
- you can practise choosing devices to present your material clearly and attractively
- you can practise using effective and interesting language in whatever you write.

Your learning

This lesson will help you to:

- gain an overview of punctuation
- understand how to use commas, full stops and capital letters correctly.

Punctuation rules

It is important to use correct punctuation. In the exam it will help to improve your grade. Here are some rules about using punctuation. Read the following passage and see how it follows the rules that appear around the text.

> Capital letters are also used for names.

> Each new sentence starts with a capital letter.

> Capital letters are used for the main words in titles

Accurate punctuation helps the reader to follow what is being said. Lynn Truss made this clear in her book 'Eats Shoots and Leaves'. She showed how inaccurate punctuation confuses the reader, creates ambiguities and is a sign of sloppy thinking. However, clear and accurate punctuation makes reading easy. Pairs of commas, showing that items placed between them are separate from the rest of the sentence, help the reader to keep the main point in mind. Although Lynn Truss's book is actually a serious book about accuracy in writing, she makes it amusing to read.

> Each sentence ends with a full stop (or question mark or exclamation mark).

> A comma is used after 'however' if it starts a sentence.

> Commas separate items in a list except for the last two which are joined by 'and'.

> Commas in pairs separate off from the rest of the sentence something which could have been put in brackets.

> A comma sometimes denotes a pause in the sentence, usually before a new clause is introduced.

Full stops and capital letters

Full stops are used at the end of a sentence. Each new sentence needs to begin with a **capital letter** and end with a full stop. Capital letters are also used for names, and for the main words in book or film titles.

Activity 1

The full stops and capital letters have been left out from the newspaper article below.

Write out the passage correctly, putting the full stops and capital letters in the right places.

you can't go anywhere in manchester at the moment the tram tracks are all up in the city centre and it's chaos you can't even get a bus to the tram either if you want to go to the lowry centre in salford quays you have to go to st peter's square and hope a tram will come someone told me the other day that it was about water pipes but i haven't seen anything about it in the press and there aren't any posters about it maybe the council thinks visitors don't count

Check your answer

GradeStudio

In your answer to Activity I:
- Did you find all 6 full stops?
- Did you find all 16 capital letters?

If not, go back and see if you can find the rest now.

Commas

Commas can be used in **four different** ways.

Method	Example
1 To separate items in a list with the last two joined by 'and' rather than a comma.	The youngster has had trials with Norwich, Leicester, Everton and Spurs.
2 Instead of brackets to separate a phrase or clause out from the rest of the sentence.	The striker, who turned 17 today, is now the youngest Premiership goal scorer of all time.
3 To make a pause, usually before a clause.	He is considered to be the brightest prospect in the game, with many big clubs tracking his progress.
4 After 'However' at the start of a sentence.	However, he is yet to be called up to the England Under 21s.

Activity 2

1 Read the four sentences below.

2 Write each sentence out again, correcting the sentences by putting commas in.

3 Write down which of the four rules about commas applies to each sentence.

> 1 A new high-speed train line which would cut travelling time drastically has been announced recently.
>
> 2 It would run from London via Birmingham Manchester Warrington Liverpool and Preston to Glasgow and Edinburgh.
>
> 3 It would only take 46 minutes from London to Birmingham with London to Manchester times almost halved to 66 minutes.
>
> 4 However it won't be at full capacity until 2024.

Check your answer

GradeStudio

In your answer to Activity 2:
- Did you correct each sentence by putting commas in?
- Did you decide which of the four rules applied to each sentence?

This extract from an autobiography has all its full stops, capital letters and commas missing. Rewrite the passage with the punctuation in place.

when i was a kid one of the most exciting and romantic things to do was to go on a train journey we lived in the potteries and i can remember going on a little branch line from stoke-on-trent to hanley through all the coal-fired factories and furnaces before we saw the slag heaps where the fuel came from the reds yellows and blues lit up the night sky and flames flashed and flared as we went through etruria much later i remember my father taking me on the first diesel train from crewe to manchester travelling through places i came to know much better as a teenager such as sandbach holmes chapel wilmslow and stockport easy journeys on time passenger comfort helpful porters and convenient connections are now things of the past leaves on the line the wrong kind of snow and operational difficulties have taken over romance and excitement have gone it makes me feel old

Check your answer

GradeStudio

In your answer to Activity 3, did you include:
- 24 capital letters
- 8 full stops
- 7 commas?

Apostrophes

Your learning

This lesson will help you to:

- understand the two main types of apostrophes
- understand how to use apostrophes correctly.

Using apostrophes

Apostrophes can be used in **two** main ways.

1 To show that a letter is missing, for example: *don't* (short for *do not*); *it's* (short for *it is*).

2 To show possession (that something belongs to someone). For example:
The Formula I car's engine is capable of producing speeds of up to 258 miles per hour.
Here the apostrophe shows that the engine belongs to the car.

Activity 1

1 Read the extract below.

> I can't help but think that I'm going to improve my punctuation skills by concentrating hard. In fact we're all going to improve. That's because we're going to be thinking about detail and because we know that we can't afford to make too many mistakes. If we don't spend time thinking about how to use apostrophes then my teacher's right: we won't improve. Hopefully by the end of this lesson I'll be using apostrophes perfectly. It's not hard, really.

Look for any words that include an apostrophe. When you find one, write it down and then write down how the full word would look if the apostrophe were not being used.

2 You could record your answer in a table.

Apostrophes of possession

The rules for apostrophes of possession are quite straightforward. Look at them below.

If something belongs to something singular (this means there is only one), then write the word, add the apostrophe and add an 's'. For example:

- *the cat's paws* – the paws belonging to one cat
- *your heart's desire* – the desire belonging to your heart
- *the class's classroom* – the classroom belonging to one class.

If something belongs to something plural (more than one) ending in 's', then write the word and add an apostrophe. For example:

- *the cats' paws* – the paws belonging to more than one cat
- *their hearts' desires* – the desires belonging to their hearts
- *the classes' classroom* – the classroom belonging to more than one class.

If something belongs to something plural which doesn't end in an 's', then write the word, add an apostrophe and add an 's'. For example:

- *the children's books* – the books belonging to the children
- *the sheep's pasture* – the pasture belonging to the sheep.

The only exception to these rules covers **possessives**. These carry the idea of possession inside them and so they don't have an apostrophe. They are: *yours*, *his*, *hers*, *its*, *theirs*, *ours*.

If you follow these simple rules, then you can't go wrong with apostrophes!

Remember, however:

its means 'belonging to it'

it's means 'it is'.

Activity 2

Put in the apostrophes where they are needed in the sentences below.

1 Its not enough just to write your answer.
2 Youve got to make sure that you check carefully.
3 Students errors often lead to their underperformance.
4 Almost every piece of work in the exam has its errors.
5 The twins faces were identical.

Question marks, exclamation marks and inverted commas

Your learning

This lesson will help you to:

- understand how to use question marks, exclamation marks and inverted commas correctly.

Question marks

A **question mark** is needed at the end of every direct question.
For example: *Where are you going?* or *Why are exams necessary?*

Exclamation marks

An exclamation is a shout, so use an **exclamation mark** when something is shouted or when something is a shock or surprise.

Some students overuse exclamation marks. One is plenty. Don't decorate the page by doubling or trebling them. If you think about the 'shout', then you will be safe. For example, *Then I fell asleep* doesn't need an exclamation mark, but *Ouch!* does.

Activity 1

1. Read the following rather informal text.
2. Put in the question marks and exclamation marks, as well as full stops and capital letters.

> women playing football do you think this is a cool idea ridiculous women should know their place and not mess with men's sports that's the view of lots of men who don't know how good women can be at football which arsenal team won this year's championship was it the men no way the women which national team made it all the way to the semi-finals of the euros this year the men or the women the fact is that women's football is the fastest growing sport and it is here to stay get over it

Check your answer

GradeStudio

In your answer to Activity I, did you put in:
- 4 full stops
- 2 exclamation marks
- 4 question marks
- 12 capital letters?

Are they all now in the right places?

Inverted commas

Inverted commas are used in two situations.

1 Around direct speech (what someone actually said).
   For example: *'What light from yonder window breaks?' asks Romeo when he is in the Capulets' garden.*

2 Around the titles of books, newspapers, magazines, films, plays, short stories or poem titles (except for the Bible and the Qur'an).
   For example: *I've been studying 'Romeo and Juliet' for my Shakespeare play.*

Activity 2

Read the passage below and put in the missing inverted commas around the titles and the direct speech.

There was a weird article the other week in the free newspaper, Metro. People take their poodles to a creative grooming parlour and get them sheared into various different shapes, such as camels, buffaloes and even horses.

Photographer Ren Netherland said It's amazing what they can do in so little time.

He is convinced that the dogs love the attention.

All the attention that gets bestowed on them must be nice for them, the photographer said.

I didn't see any report of this story in broadsheet papers such as The Financial Times.

Check your answer

GradeStudio

In your answer to Activity 2:
- Did you find the two newspaper titles?
- Did you find the two quotations?

Assessment practice

Your learning

This lesson will help you to:

- practise an exam-style question
- assess your answer by looking at other responses.

Activity 1

Spend 15 minutes writing about what kinds of people become celebrities and what you think of them. Make sure you give some specific examples.

1 Think about what kinds of people become celebrities. Are celebrities always people with a particular talent or skill? Are there different types of celebrities?

2 Now think about the celebrities you know and write down their names.

Then write:

- what you like about them
- what you dislike about them.

You could write down your ideas in the form of a spider diagram.

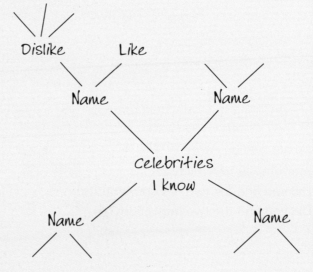

3 Number all your points so that they come in the right order and form groups that will make paragraphs.

4 When you are writing, make sure that you:
- use accurate punctuation
- use a range of different punctuation marks.

5 When you have finished, check your work carefully for accuracy and make any changes you need to.

Peer/Self-assessment activity

1 Check your answer to the assessment activity. Did you:
   - answer the question all the time
   - say what you thought about specific people
   - make sure your paragraphs followed each other
   - use a range of different punctuation marks
   - check your punctuation for accuracy?

2 Now grade your answer using the mark scheme below. First, read the sample answers to this task on pages 146–147.

   Examiners have to give two separate marks for your writing, but here you are just concentrating on the punctuation.

G
   ▶ some punctuation

F
   ▶ occasional full stops

E
   ▶ some accurate sentence demarcation
   ▶ accuracy in more than just full stops

D
   ▶ starts to use range of punctuation

C
   ▶ generally secure in punctuation

Here are two student answers to the activity on pages 144–145. Read the answers together with the examiner comments, and then complete the final peer/self-assessment task.

Student A

Celebrities are people who everyone knows and knows about because they are famous maybe they are pop singers or footballers or people in the media the best celebrities are those who get up to no good or are always in the media because of the things they have done like beaten somebody up outside a club or fallen down in the street drunk because they are a politician the one I like best is Katie Price aka Jordan because she is always in the media and always having trouble with her ex peter Andray and I like her tv programmes because they are always interesting and always have lots of drama in them I don't like peter Andray because he left her with his children and although there are always pictures in the paper of him giving his kids a good time these are because he wants the media to like him and people reading the papers and watching tv to like him.

Apostrophe used correctly.

Full stop at the end.

Examiner comment

This student has a lot to say and has answered the question by explaining what sort of people become celebrities and giving her views on two of them. She knows a lot about her two chosen celebrities and has included a bit of detail, but in terms of punctuation it is weak. She can use the apostrophe correctly (which suggests that she knows about punctuation) and there is a full stop at the end, but that is all. She is probably enthusiastic about writing about this topic and therefore forgets to plan, forgets to use paragraphs and forgets about her punctuation most of the time. In terms of punctuation, this falls into the G band.

Student B

Correct full stop.

Correct exclamation mark.

Correct capital letters for names.

Correct commas used instead of brackets.

Correct question mark.

Correct apostrophe.

Correct apostrophe.

Celebrities used to be people who had done something important and were therefore in the public eye. Not any more! Celebrities can be anyone who is in the papers a lot. So people with very little talent, such as Katie Price and Peter Andre, are called celebrities even though they haven't done anything very useful or interesting. I think celebrities nowadays are people who entertain the general public.

Who do I like? I admire Esther Rantzen for sticking up for what she believes in when it's unfashionable. I admire Paula Ratcliffe for her sporting achievements. I admire Tony Benn for bringing fresh air to politics even when he's retired.

Correct capital letters for names.

Examiner comment

This uses a range of punctuation marks, all correctly. It is certainly in the C range.

Use accurate punctuation

Higher marks will be given to answers which use a range of punctuation marks and use them correctly.

Make sure that you use at least three different kinds of punctuation in your Writing task, and make sure that you check each one carefully when you have finished writing.

Putting it into practice

Explain what you now know about:
- using punctuation marks
- using a range of punctuation
- checking your work for accuracy
- what makes the difference between Grade G and C answers in terms of punctuation.

In the future:

- you can practise looking at correct punctuation in whatever you read
- you can practise using a range of punctuation
- you can practise checking your own work for accurate punctuation.

Use accurate sp

It is important to try to spell as accurately as possible in the exam.
This means you have to read what you have written and check it for accuracy.

Activity 1

It is sometimes easier to find spelling mistakes in what other people have written than in your own work.

Read the following extract written by a student.

1 Find **ten** spelling mistakes.

2 Look up the correct spellings in a dictionary.

3 Start a spelling notebook. Write words that you often misspell in it.

> Celebrities are people who are famous for doing somthing. There people who are often in the media becos of what has happened to them and becaus people want to read about them. Jordan is someone the media love to hate. She's always in the news, wether it's for getting drunk when she's out clubing or haveing another argument with Peter Andre. She mite be in it just for the money or to make sure the public doesn't forget about her. Watever the reason, it's dissapointing that the media seem to pick on her.

Check your answer

GradeStudio

In your answer to Activity 1:

- Did you find all ten mistakes?
- Did you find the same word spelt two different ways (both wrongly)?
- Did you write down the correct spellings?

Most words obey the two rules below, although there are a few exceptions.

Rule I
i before e except after c if the sound is 'ee'.
For example, *perceive* not *percieve*.

Rule 2
If you are making an adverb, you write the word and add 'ly' to it.
For example: *loving + ly = lovingly*.

Activity 2

1 Use Rule I to decide which spelling of the following words is correct:

A	piece	or	peice
B	seige	or	siege
C	deceive	or	decieve
D	recieve	or	receive

2 Use Rule 2 to decide which spelling of the following words is correct:

A	calmly	or	calmlly
B	eventually	or	eventualy
C	beautifuly	or	beautifully
D	realy	or	really
E	securely	or	securly

3 Now look at the following text and find **eight** spelling mistakes. Write out the correct spellings for each one.

I think that the X Factor has gone too far. It used to be realy good when in the first round the contestents had to sing on their own to the judges without music, but now they have to recieve the cheers and boos of a big audeince. Some can't sing at all, even though they think they have sung their peice beautifuly and the audience behaves realy badley, callouslly booing them.

Check your answer

In your answer to Activity 2:
- Did you find all eight mistakes?
- Did you look up any words you were uncertain about?
- Did you write them in your spelling notebook?

GradeStudio

Use accurate spelling

Here are some words which students often misspell:

beautiful   sincerely
because   fulfil
whether   receive

And here are some words which students muddle up:

there (in that place)	and	they're (they are)
its (belonging to it)	and	it's (it is)
weather (the climate)	and	whether (should I?)

Activity 3

1 Read the following text and choose which spelling should be used in place of each number.

(1) not hard to write accurately if you work at your (2) and learn a few words a day. You (3) get high marks in the exam if you don't write as (4) as you can and if you forget to check your work (5) when you have finished (6). (7) are many mistakes (8) are made (9) students are thinking about what (10) (11) rather than how (12) (13) it.

1   its or it's

2   speling or spelling

3   carn't or can't

4   accurately or accuratly

5   carefuly or carefully

6   writeing or writing

7   their or there

8   witch or which

9   because or becos

10   there or they're

11   writting or writing

12   there or they're

13   writting or writing

Assessment practice

Peer/Self-assessment activity

> **Your learning**
>
> **This lesson will help you to:**
>
> - practise an exam-style question
> - assess your answer by looking at other responses.

Activity 1

Now spend about 10 minutes writing your own text.

Choose something you know a lot about and explain why you are interested in it.

Use as wide a range of interesting words as you can, but concentrate on your spelling.

When you have finished:

- look carefully at your spellings
- use a dictionary to correct any mistakes you think you might have made
- write down any words you misspelt in your spelling notebook.

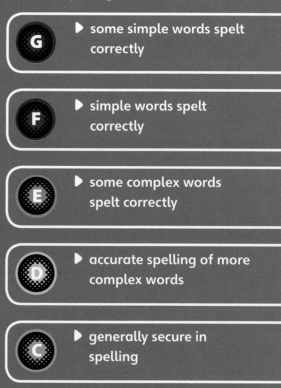

1 Check your answer to the assessment activity. Did you:
- find your spelling errors
- use a dictionary
- add any words to your spelling notebook?

2 Now grade your answer using the mark scheme below. First, read the sample answers to this task on pages 152–153.

Examiners have to give two separate marks for your writing, but here you are just concentrating on the spelling.

G ▶ some simple words spelt correctly

F ▶ simple words spelt correctly

E ▶ some complex words spelt correctly

D ▶ accurate spelling of more complex words

C ▶ generally secure in spelling

Here are three student answers to the activity on page 151. Read the answers together with the examiner comments, and then complete the final peer/self-assessment task.

the activity on page 151

F grade answer

Student A

Very simple words spelt incorrectly.

Very simple words spelt incorrectly.

Wen I leve skool I what to luk afta aminals. I begun to be intrested in aminals wen my parants brung mee a pupy home and I have now lukt affter him for ate years. I lik groming him and making him look gud. Wen he luks gud he fells gud to and I can tel becos he nuzels me and cudeles me. I offen take him for warks. He luvs his ecsersize and will run and run untill hes tyred and we hav to go hoam.

Examiner comment

This student can spell very simple words correctly but has problems with words more than three letters long. The only slightly longer words spelt correctly here are 'years' and 'making' .On spelling this answer falls just at the bottom of the F band.

E grade answer

Student B

A more complex word spelt correctly.

Misspellings of simple words.

A more complex word spelt correctly.

Complex word spelt incorrectly.

When I leave school I want to look after animals. I began to be intrested in animals when my parents brung me a puppy home and I have now looked after him for eight years. I like grooming him and making him look good. When he looks good he feels good to and I can tell becos he nuzels me and cuddles me. I often take him for walks. He loves his ecsersize and will run and run until he's tired and we have to go home.

Examiner comment

This student does not use many complex words but has managed to spell two correctly. However, other complex words and simpler words are spelt incorrectly, for example 'interested' and 'because'. On spelling this answer falls in the E band.

Student C

When I leave school I want to look after animals. I began to be interested in animals when my parents brought me a puppy home and I have now looked after him for eight years. I like grooming him and making him look good. When he looks good he feels good too and I can tell because he nuzzles me and cuddles me. I often take him for walks. He loves his exersize and will run and run until he's tired and we have to go home.

Misspelling.

Examiner comment

This student doesn't use many complex words, but all except one are spelt correctly. A C-grade student would normally use a wider vocabulary than this, and a wider range of more complex words, but the spelling of all the commonly used words is accurate and so for spelling it falls just into the C band.

Use accurate spelling

Higher marks will be given to answers which use a range of interesting words with accurate spelling.

Make sure that you keep your spelling notebook going throughout your course, so that you can be confident about your spelling when it comes to the exam.

Don't forget to check your work very carefully for spelling when you think you've finished your writing tasks.

Putting it into practice

Explain what you now know about:
- spelling accurately
- checking your work carefully for spelling
- what makes the difference between Grade F, E and C answers in terms of spelling.

In the future:

- you can practise looking at correct spellings in whatever you read
- you can practise spelling a range of words correctly
- you can practise checking your own work for accurate spelling.

Use a range of sentence structures

Look back to page 54 for a reminder of the four basic kinds of sentence that are frequently used.

Simple sentences

A **simple sentence** has a subject and one verb. For example:

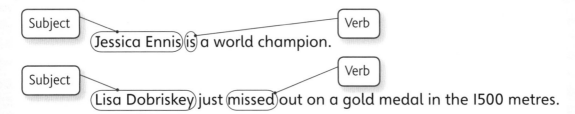

Activity 1

Simple sentences are often used in information texts for children.

1 Read the passage about dinosaurs opposite, written for children.

Did you notice that:

- these are all simple sentences
- each sentence starts with a capital letter
- each sentence ends with a full stop?

2 Now write for 10 minutes, giving information for children about a topic you are interested in. Use only simple sentences.

Dinosaurs

Dinosaurs were early forms of reptiles. They lived between 240 and 65 million years ago. There were many different kinds of dinosaur. They all lived on dry land. None of them could fly. Animals such as crocodiles and sharks also lived at the same time as dinosaurs. There were also flying reptiles. Some huge reptiles lived in the sea. Dinosaurs laid their eggs in a nest. Some buried them. They were too big to sit on without crushing them.

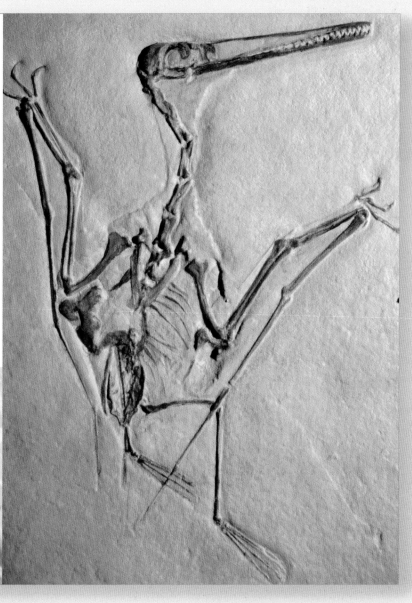

GradeStudio

Check your answer

In your answer to Activity I:
- Did you give your piece a title?
- Did you use only simple sentences?
- Did you start each sentence with a capital letter?
- Did you end each sentence with a full stop?

Compound sentences

A **compound sentence** is two simple sentences joined together with a conjunction (such as 'and', 'or', 'but'). For example:

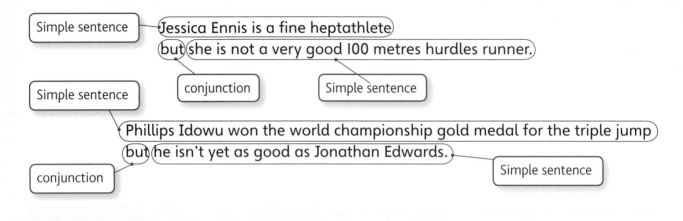

Activity 2

1 For each of the sentences in the following passage, write down whether you think it is a simple sentence or a compound sentence using a table like the one below.

2 If it is a compound sentence, write down the conjunction. Each sentence has a number at the end that you can use in your answers.

> Some dinosaurs were very big but some were small. (1) The biggest dinosaur bone belonged to Amphicoelias fragillimus. (2) This dinosaur might have been 60 metres long. (3) One of the smallest was Compsognathus. (4) It was about sixty centimetres long and was a fast-running hunter. (5) Some dinosaurs swallowed stones called gastroliths. (6) These rubbed together and helped to grind down the food. (7) Hadrosaurs had two or three rows of teeth at the back of their jaws but none at the front. (8) They could rub their teeth together in different directions and this enabled them to grind and grate their food. (9)

	Type of sentence	Conjunction
1	compound	but

3 Now rewrite the passage on dinosaurs from Activity I on page 155, so that you link some of the simple sentences with a conjunction.

Check your answer

In your answer to Activity 2:
- Did you use some conjunctions?
- Did you start each sentence with a capital letter?
- Did you end each sentence with a full stop?

Activity 3

Look back at the writing you did in Activity I on page 154, where you used simple sentences. Rewrite this so that it uses a mixture of simple and compound sentences.

Check your answer

In your answer to Activity 3:
- Did you give your piece a title?
- Did you start every sentence with a capital letter?
- Did you end every sentence with a full stop?

Complex and minor sentences

Your learning

This lesson will help you to:

- use complex sentences
- use a range of sentence structures and forms for effect.

Complex sentences

A **complex sentence** is a longer sentence where one part is dependent on another (using what is called a **subordinating conjunction** such as 'although', 'because', 'until'). Look at the complex sentence below.

(When) I arrived, I saw that things were worse than I could possibly have imagined.

conjunction   use of comma to link the two parts

Activity 1

Complex sentences use subordinating conjunctions to link ideas together in a sentence. Look at the examples of subordinating conjunctions below.

because	although	even though	despite	so	as
which	who	if	when	until	

1   Here are five pairs of simple sentences. Join each pair by using one of the conjunctions in the table above so that you make it into a complex sentence.

> 1   I was just ready to go out. The telephone rang.
> 2   My sister rang. She wanted me to do her a favour.
> 3   I didn't want to do it. I hate babysitting.
> 4   Her little daughter is a demon. She is always getting up to mischief.
> 5   I had to do it. I needed the money.

2   Now look at the dinosaur passage on page 155 again and turn some of the sentences into complex sentences, so that you end up with a mixture of simple, compound and complex sentences.

Check your answer

GradeStudio

In your answer to Activity 1, have you made sure that:

- every sentence begins with a capital letter
- every sentence ends with a full stop
- you now have simple, compound and complex sentences in the passage?

Minor sentences

Another type of sentence is the **minor sentence**. It isn't really a sentence at all, because it is just one or two words on their own. It's used for dramatic effect, to make the reader sit up and take notice.

For example, a writer can follow a long sentence with a very short minor sentence.

After such a close and exciting match it was disappointing that my hero served a double fault on match point. Gutted!

minor sentence

After all that preparation he arrived on the blocks after the false start of the semi-final and set off before the gun had gone off. Disqualification.

Activity 2

Now it is time to put your learning about the different kinds of sentences to use.

1. Choose a sport or hobby which you enjoy and spend 10 minutes writing one or two paragraphs telling the reader all about it.

   Your main task here is to write a mixture of simple, compound and complex sentences. If you can, include some minor sentences for effect.

   This means you need to work out what you are going to say before you start to write, so that you can concentrate on constructing your sentences as you are writing.

2. When you have finished, label each of your sentences to show whether it is simple, compound or complex.

Activity 1

Write an article for a teenage magazine, persuading readers not to smoke.

Spend:

- 5 minutes making a plan and sequencing your points
- 15 minutes writing
- 5 minutes checking your sentences.

Remember to:

- write a heading
- make a list of your ideas
- sequence your points by numbering them
- decide on your paragraphs.

Peer/Self-assessment activity

1 Check your answer to the assessment activity. Did you:
   - remember the heading
   - make sure you answered the question all the time
   - put your points in the best order
   - use paragraphs
   - check your sentences for accuracy
   - use a mixture of simple, compound, complex and minor sentences for effect?

2 Now grade your answer using the mark scheme below. First, read the sample answers to this task on pages 162–163. Examiners have to give two separate marks for your writing in the exam. For this activity just concentrate on the descriptors for sentences and sentence structures.

G ▸ some sentences

F ▸ mainly simple and compound sentences

E ▸ generally accurate sentence demarcation

D ▸ range of securely demarcated sentences

C ▸ uses sentence forms for effect

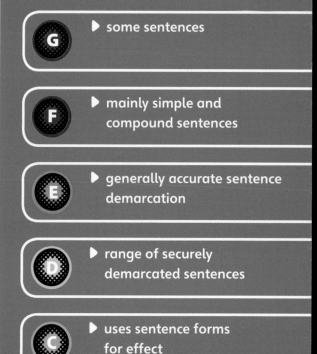

Here are three student answers to the activity on pages 160–161. Read the answers together with the examiner comments, and then complete the final peer/self-assessment task.

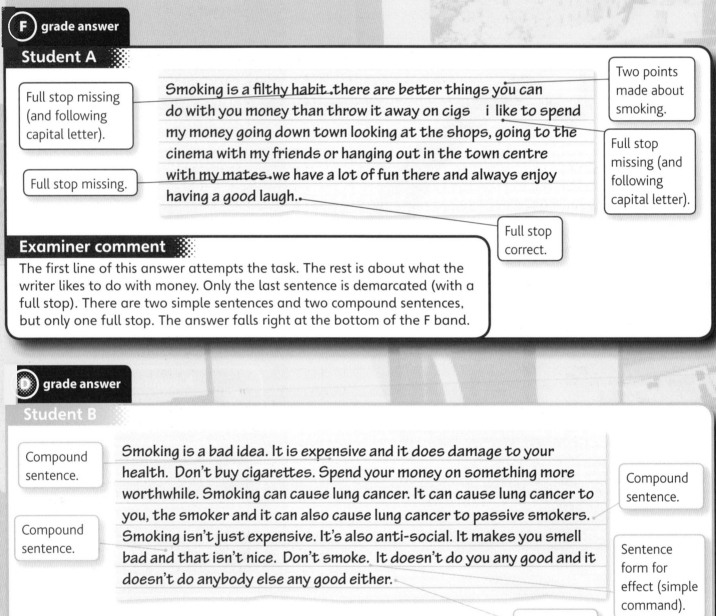

F grade answer

Student A

Full stop missing (and following capital letter).

Full stop missing.

Smoking is a filthy habit.there are better things you can do with you money than throw it away on cigs   i like to spend my money going down town looking at the shops, going to the cinema with my friends or hanging out in the town centre with my mates.we have a lot of fun there and always enjoy having a good laugh..

Two points made about smoking.

Full stop missing (and following capital letter).

Full stop correct.

Examiner comment

The first line of this answer attempts the task. The rest is about what the writer likes to do with money. Only the last sentence is demarcated (with a full stop). There are two simple sentences and two compound sentences, but only one full stop. The answer falls right at the bottom of the F band.

D grade answer

Student B

Compound sentence.

Compound sentence.

Smoking is a bad idea. It is expensive and it does damage to your health. Don't buy cigarettes. Spend your money on something more worthwhile. Smoking can cause lung cancer. It can cause lung cancer to you, the smoker and it can also cause lung cancer to passive smokers. Smoking isn't just expensive. It's also anti-social. It makes you smell bad and that isn't nice. Don't smoke. It doesn't do you any good and it doesn't do anybody else any good either.

Compound sentence.

Sentence form for effect (simple command).

Compound sentence.

Examiner comment

This answer uses four compound sentences. The rest are all simple sentences. There are no complex sentences or minor sentences. However, all sentences are accurately demarcated. This gives the examiner a bit of a problem, because although there is one sentence form for effect (a touch of a C) and although the sentences are securely demarcated (a clear C but no range), there are only simple and compound sentences (F). Overall, then, this falls on the D/E boundary.

Student C

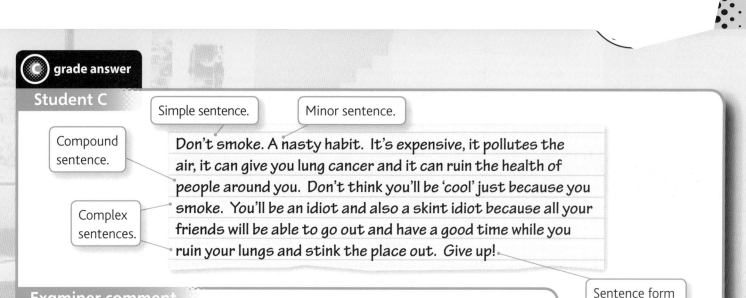

Compound sentence.

Simple sentence.

Minor sentence.

Complex sentences.

Don't smoke. A nasty habit. It's expensive, it pollutes the air, it can give you lung cancer and it can ruin the health of people around you. Don't think you'll be 'cool' just because you smoke. You'll be an idiot and also a skint idiot because all your friends will be able to go out and have a good time while you ruin your lungs and stink the place out. Give up!

Sentence form for effect.

Examiner comment

This is a short and undeveloped answer, but everything is relevant to the topic and it uses all four kinds of sentence structure effectively, although some of them only once. All sentences are correctly demarcated. In terms of sentence structures it falls clearly into the C band.

MOVING UP THE GRADES

Use a range of sentence structures

Higher marks will be given to answers that have a variety of sentence structures to maintain the interest of the reader.

So, thinking about what kind of sentence you use, and varying the length and construction of the sentence, is important in gaining the highest grades.

Making sure that you have the correct punctuation mark at the end of each sentence is also important.

Putting it into practice

Explain what you now know about:
- using different kinds of sentences
- using sentence forms for effect
- demarcating your sentences correctly
- what makes the difference between Grade F, D and C answers on the using a range of sentence structures.

In the future:

- you can practise finding the four different kinds of sentences
- you can practise using all four of them
- you can practise checking that you have the correct punctuation mark at the end of every sentence.

English/English Language

(Specification A)
FOUNDATION

Unit 1 Understanding and producing non-fiction texts

Answer **all** questions   **Time allowed**
                              • 2 hours

Section A: Reading

Answer **all** questions

You are advised to spend about one hour on this section.

Read Item 1, *Fun Run Conman* and answer the questions below.

1 Why did Alan Rawsthorne claim disability benefit?   *(4 marks)*

2 What was the case against Brian Rawsthorne?   *(4 marks)*

Read Item 2 *...and how did our 5ft 4in Tadpole become the best woman athlete in the world?* and answer the question below.

3 What, according to the article, is the key to Jessica Ennis's success?   *(8 marks)*

Read Item 3, *Explained: Blu-ray* and answer the question below.

4 How are presentational devices used on this page to make it interesting and effective?   *(12 marks)*

Look again at Item 1, *Fun Run Conman*, and Item 2 … *and how did our 5ft 4in Tadpole become the best woman athlete in the world?* and answer the question below.

5 Compare the effect on the reader of some of the choices of language and presentational devices.   *(12 marks)*

Section B: Writing

Answer **both** questions in this section.

You are advised to spend about one hour on this section.

---

1 Write a letter to the editor of the *Daily Mirror* explaining why you think the government should still support people who are unemployed and disabled. *(16 marks)*

2 The Prince's Trust is organising a competition to find out about the people young people admire. Choose someone you admire. Give some information about your chosen person and explain why you admire him or her. *(24 marks)*

Item 1

Daily Mirror

FUN RUN CONMAN

Dad runs 10k while claiming £12k in disability benefit

A BENEFITS cheat who claimed he could only walk 20 yards was caught – after doing a 10k fun run.

Brian Rawsthorne pocketed over £12,000 in Disability Living Allowance and continued to claim even after competing in the BUPA Great Manchester run last year.

The 50-year-old, who ran the 10k course in two hours, eight minutes, denied failing to notify the Department for Work and Pensions of a change in circumstances.

But Manchester magistrates found him guilty after they were shown news footage of him taking part in the run. Rawsthorne, who raised £1,000 in the race, had told a newspaper he had lost over two stone training for the May event.

They were also shown a TV documentary of the dad-of-two running when the race started.

Prosecutor Paul Darnborough said, 'The Department would say his ability to cope with his disability is a change in circumstances.' The court heard, Rawsthorne, an ex-miner, had been the sole survivor of an explosion that killed 10 men at Golborne Colliery, near Wigan, in 1979. It left him with severe burns and lung damage.

He began claiming disability benefits in 1997 – saying he sometimes walked using crutches. DWP officials began an investigation after they got a tip-off he was refereeing football matches.

But Rawsthorne, of Newton Heath, Manchester, denied the charges. He said: 'There's still no change. I cannot walk 20 yards without pain.' He received a six-month conditional discharge and was told to repay the benefit money.

BY STEPHEN WHITE
s.white@mirror.co.uk

Item 2

...and how did our 5ft 4in Tadpole become the best woman athlete in the world?

She may be just 5ft 4in tall and weigh less than 9st, but over the weekend British heptathlete Jessica Ennis showed the athletics world size doesn't always matter.

The 23-year-old from Yorkshire overcame injury (she fractured her ankle in two places last year) to dominate the World Championships, not only taking the gold but leaving her rivals trailing far behind.

From being virtually unknown 48 hours ago, she's now being hailed as one of the most remarkable sportswomen in the world – and hot favourite as Sports Personality Of The Year.

Her achievements are even more inspiring given her size.

The heptathlon – which involves 100m hurdles, 200m sprint, the high jump, the long jump, the shotput, the javelin and an 800m run – traditionally suits the taller athlete, but The Tadpole (as one rival nicknamed her) has morphed into one of the world's leading all-round athletes.

Sports expert Professor Jo Doust, chairman of the British Association of Sports and Exercise Science, says that while Jessica is five inches shorter and around a stone and a half lighter than most of her competitors, she makes up for it with her power-to-weight ratio.

'For her body size, she's very powerful,' he adds. 'Her body is low in fat but her muscles are very developed.'

This may be down to her strict diet and six-day-a-week exercise plan. On a daily basis, she needs to consume a high-protein, high-carbohydrate diet to give her energy. She starts the day with a bowl of bran flakes with fruit, yoghurt and orange juice, followed by a wholemeal ham salad sandwich for lunch and chilli and rice or pasta and chicken for dinner. She snacks on cereal bars and bananas, but also Haribo sweets and Jelly Babies for the sugar and professes a love for chocolate.

This dedication to her sport has been growing since childhood. Jessica joined the City of Sheffield athletics club in 1998, aged just 11. By 16 she was taking part in international junior contests. She burst on to the senior scene in 2005 when her performance in the Turkish Universiade saw her steal the bronze medal from under the noses of seasoned professionals – despite the fact she was also studying for a psychology degree.

Her personal best in the high jump is a huge 1.95m, making her one of only ten women to have jumped 30cm above their own height.

She was a medal hope for the 2008 Olympics, but a fractured ankle put her dreams on hold. She fought back to fitness (including learning to take off for the long jump from her other foot to protect her right ankle), and has since improved on her personal best, jumping an astounding 6.43m in an event last month.

But Professor Doust believes her real skills lie in her ability as an all-rounder – she works hard even at her weakest events so her overall scores never flag. So having run, jumped, thrown and put her way to the world No.1 spot, it seems all that hard work has finally paid off. Bring on 2012!

JENNY STOCKS

Item 3

Explained

Charting the shifting currents of modern culture

Blu-ray

If you want to get the most out of your high-definition TV, you need to feed it high-definition images. Since February 2008, the only domestic high-definition disc has been Blu-ray. Sure, we've all heard of it — you may already own a player— but for the rest of us is there *really* any difference, and is it worth the money?

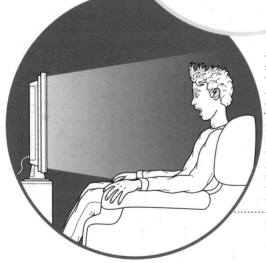

What does Blu-ray do? Blu-ray discs look the same as standard DVDs, but they're not. A DVD player will not play a Blu-ray disc, although a Blu-ray player will typically play all disc formats. Blu-ray images are four or five times crisper and clearer than DVD. To get the most out of a Blu-ray player, your TV should be able to play high-definition in 1080 format. Think of 1080 as the number of lines on your screen, and you won't go far wrong.

How does it work? Blu-ray uses, unsurprisingly, a blue laser ray to read discs, instead of the standard red of a DVD. For complex reasons to do with light wavelength and better focus, this allows more information to be crammed on to a disc, resulting in better picture and sound.

So are my DVDs obsolete? Not at all. Blu-ray looks best with modern films, and its high level of detail can even expose flaws in older titles. On the new James Bond Blu-rays you can clearly see that it is stuntman Bob Simmons, not Sean Connery, who fires the gun in the opening sequence, something that was not apparent even in the cinema.

Should I buy one? If you're looking to replace a DVD player, the simple answer is why not? Prices have fallen to around £160 and Blu-ray still beats on-demand downloading (via Sky, BT Vision and the like) since HD is delivered via 720 format, rather than Blu-Ray's supercrisp 1080 format.
Nigel Kendall

STEVE DAVIS

March 14-20, 2009 | Playlist | **11**